LASTING TOXIC RELATIONSHIP RECOVERY

How to End the Cycle, Live Authentically, Love Fully, and Rediscover Yourself

---

LESLIE AND KIM GOWANS

To my sister, Cana,

Your bravery in leaving a toxic relationship has profoundly inspired everyone around you. For over a decade, you've poured your heart into healing yourself and nurturing your precious daughter, demonstrating remarkable resilience and rediscovery. Your journey stands as a powerful testament to love, strength, and unwavering determination.

This book is dedicated to you and to all those courageous individuals who reclaim their lives and embrace authenticity. May your story continue to inspire and illuminate the path for others on their own journeys.

With all my love and admiration,
Leslie

Free Workbook +

Table of Contents

Introduction

Do you feel like you're constantly walking on eggshells, drained by the emotional turmoil that seems to shadow your every relationship move? If you nod, know you're not alone in this struggle. Many of us have faced the confusion and pain of toxic relationships, all the while holding on to the hope for genuine love and happiness. This universal desire to break free and find an authentic connection inspired me to write "Toxic Relationship Recovery: How to End the Cycle, Rediscover Yourself, and Love Authentically." This book is more than just a guide; it's a roadmap to emotional liberation and self-discovery.

My journey, like yours, was riddled with moments of doubt and despair, tied down by relationships that promised love but delivered pain. I remember the days when I felt I could never escape the cycle of negativity, constantly questioning my self-worth and ability to find a peaceful, loving partnership. Sharing these experiences isn't easy, but I do it in hopes that you might see a reflection of your own life and realize that change is not just possible—it's attainable.

Understanding what makes a relationship toxic is our starting point. Throughout this book, we explore various facets of toxic interactions, which are not limited to romantic entanglements but can also include platonic, familial, and professional relationships. By recognizing these patterns, you can begin to take steps toward healthier connections.

This book's blend of personal narrative, psychological insights, and practical advice sets it apart. I've woven together my own experiences with research-backed strategies to offer a comprehensive path to healing. Whether you're just beginning to question the health of your relationships or ready to take significant steps toward change, this guide will equip you with the necessary knowledge wherever you are in your journey.

This book is for anyone who has ever felt underestimated or overpowered within a relationship. It doesn't matter if you're young or old, male or female, or somewhere in between; if you're seeking a way out of toxicity and eager to step into a life of authentic, fulfilling love, you are the reader I'm speaking to.

I've structured the book to help you understand and identify toxic dynamics, heal from past hurts, and empower you to establish and nurture authentic relationships. Each chapter builds on the last, creating a supportive scaffold that grows with your understanding and emotional strength.

An essential part of this journey is the self-work required to achieve personal growth and healing. With each page, I aim to guide you through this reflective process with empathy and actionable steps, ensuring you have the tools to thrive, not just survive.

So, as you turn these pages, remember that each step forward is a step towards a life filled with healthier relationships and a more profound love for yourself and others. You have the strength to break the cycle of toxicity. Let this book be your companion as you step into a world where you can live and love authentically and wholeheartedly. Embrace this journey—you are worth it.

ONE

Understanding Toxic Relationships

Have you ever felt that every argument leaves you questioning your thoughts and feelings? It's a common thread among those who have endured toxic relationships, where the line between normal disagreements and harmful interactions often seems blurred. This chapter is dedicated to unraveling the complexities of toxic relationships, moving beyond the surface-level signs to a deeper understanding of the patterns and impacts that define them. Here, we'll dissect what makes a relationship challenging and genuinely toxic. We'll explore the various forms of toxic behavior, understand the profound effects they can have on individuals, and learn how to distinguish between genuinely toxic traits and the usual ups and downs of relationships.

1.1 Defining Toxic Relationships: Beyond the Basics

Defining what exactly constitutes a toxic relationship can be as complex as the dynamics it describes. At its core, a toxic relationship is one that consistently leaves you feeling drained, diminished, or devalued. Unlike typical relationship conflicts that have the potential for resolution through communication and compromise, toxic relationships are marked by patterns of behavior that are deeply harmful and often escalate over time. These behaviors can include manipulation, where one person exerts undue influence over the feelings or actions of another; severe dependency, where one partner's emotional or physical needs consistently overshadow the other's; and various forms of abuse, ranging from overt physical aggression to subtle psychological control.

Toxic behaviors can manifest in many forms. Emotional toxicity might involve persistent criticism, gaslighting, or emotional blackmail, where love and affection are conditional or used as weapons. Physical toxicity, though often more visible, includes any form of bodily harm or intimidation. In contrast, psychological toxicity might involve tactics like isolation from friends and family, threats, or consistent undermining of one's self-esteem. These behaviors can erode the foundations of trust and respect that healthy relationships are built on.

The impact of being in a toxic relationship can be devastating. In the short term, victims may experience intense stress, anxiety, or a pervasive sense of fear or sadness. Long-term effects can be even more severe, leading to chronic anxiety, depression, or PTSD. These emotional and psychological wounds can profoundly affect a person's ability to trust others and themselves, potentially hindering future relationships and personal growth.

A particularly concerning trend is the mislabeling of regular relational conflicts as toxic. It's crucial to distinguish between a genuinely poisonous relationship and the typical challenges that couples may face. While consistent patterns of harmful behavior characterize toxic relationships, everyday relational conflicts are usually isolated incidents that can be resolved through healthy communication. Understanding this difference is vital in preventing the unnecessary termination of salvageable relationships and focusing energy on addressing genuinely toxic dynamics.

Interactive Element: Reflective Question

Consider the last significant conflict you experienced in a relationship:

- Did the conflict resolve with mutual understanding and respect, or did it leave you feeling diminished and powerless?
- Reflect on whether your relationship exhibits isolated conflicts or ongoing patterns that match the toxic behaviors described.

Understanding these distinctions and the true nature of toxic relationships will better equip you to make informed decisions about your relationships, distinguishing between those that deserve your effort to resolve conflicts and those that may be inherently harmful. Recognizing these patterns is the first step toward healing and eventually fostering healthier, more fulfilling connections.

1.2 Psychological Profiles of Toxic Partners

Understanding the psychological makeup of individuals who exhibit toxic behaviors in relationships can be crucial in recognizing and addressing these dynamics effectively. Personality disorders such as narcissism, borderline personality disorder (BPD), and antisocial personality disorder often underpin many of the destructive behaviors seen in toxic relationships. Narcissism is characterized by an inflated sense of one's importance, a deep need for excessive attention and admiration, and a lack of empathy for others. When this trait is present in a relationship, it may manifest as controlling behavior, constant belittling of the partner, or an inability to consider the partner's needs and feelings.

Borderline personality disorder, another significant marker within toxic relationship dynamics, includes symptoms such as emotional instability, intense episodes of anger, depression, anxiety, and an acute fear of abandonment. This can lead to impulsive actions and unstable relationships where the individual might idealize their partner one moment and devalue them the next, creating a persistent sense of insecurity and unpredictability. Antisocial personality disorder is marked by a disregard for other people's rights, with sufferers often manipulating or treating others harshly without expressing guilt. In relationships, this can translate into outright psychological and physical abuse.

These personality disorders are linked to specific toxic behaviors through various mechanisms. For instance, the narcissist's need for control and admiration might lead them to isolate their partner from friends and family, a common tactic that ensures the partner's dependence on them. Similarly, the impulsivity characteristic of BPD can result in explosive arguments and reconciliation cycles that confuse and exhaust their partners. The manipulation typical of antisocial personality disorder might manifest as gaslighting, where the partner's reality is continually undermined, leaving them doubting their sanity.

Consider the case of Alex and Jordan (names and details are altered for privacy). Alex, exhibiting clear narcissistic traits, would often dismiss Jordan's achievements while exaggerating his own. This constant undermining eroded Jordan's self-esteem, a typical outcome in such dynamics. On occasions when Jordan attempted to discuss this behavior, Alex would shift the focus of the conversation to his own feelings of being underappreciated, a classic diversion tactic in narcissistic relationships.

When dealing with individuals who exhibit these toxic traits, preliminary advice would focus on setting firm boundaries. It is essential to clearly communicate what is acceptable and what isn't and stick to these limits. Engaging in open conversations about the impact of their behavior can sometimes prompt recognition and change, but one must be prepared for resistance. Often, professional intervention in the form of therapy might be necessary — both for the individual displaying toxic behaviors and their partner. Recognizing when professional help is needed is critical in preventing further emotional damage and beginning the healing process.

1.3 Self-Assessment: Identifying Your Role in Toxic Dynamics

Recognizing one's own role in perpetuating or enabling toxic dynamics within relationships is a crucial step toward healing and breaking free from these unhealthy patterns. It starts with a deep, often uncomfortable journey into self-awareness where you must confront not just the actions of others but also reflect on your own behaviors and responses. Many of us, without realizing it, contribute to the maintenance of toxic dynamics through patterns of behavior that we've adopted over time, possibly as coping mechanisms or because they are what we've come to see as normal. For instance, codependency, where you might find yourself constantly sacrificing your needs and wants to appease your partner or poor boundary setting involves not clearly communicating your limits and allowing others to overstep them repeatedly. There's also denial—a common but destructive response, where acknowledging the reality of the situation is avoided, often to preserve the peace out of fear of being alone.

These behaviors, while they might seem as if they're keeping the peace or even helping the relationship, are in fact, doing just the opposite. They reinforce the toxic cycle, giving it space and power to thrive. Not setting boundaries inadvertently teaches your partner that their harmful actions are acceptable. By prioritizing their needs over your own, you may diminish your self-worth and perpetuate a dynamic of inequality. Understanding these patterns is the first step; actively working to change them is what ultimately alters the course of your relationship dynamics.

Self-assessment tools such as journals and reflective questionnaires can be beneficial in aiding this transformative process. These tools encourage you to engage regularly with your thoughts and feelings, track behavioral patterns, and reflect on your emotional responses to different situations. For instance, maintaining a daily journal where you record instances when you felt belittled, angry, happy, or sad can help you identify triggers and the circumstances that lead to unhealthy interactions. Reflective questionnaires can prompt deeper introspection about why you react in specific ways and how you might be enabling or sustaining toxicity without realizing it.

Let's consider an everyday example that illustrates the importance of recognizing one's role in a toxic dynamic. Imagine you're in a relationship where your partner often dismisses your opinions. Initially, you might respond by trying to argue your point more forcefully. Over time, however, you find it easier to stay quiet to avoid conflict. In this scenario, journaling about these interactions could reveal a pattern of avoidance and submission, highlighting a need to work on assertiveness and boundary-setting. Similarly, a questionnaire might ask, "How often do you find yourself giving up what you want to avoid disagreements?" Answering this honestly can be a turning point in handling such situations.

Changing one's behavior in response to this self-awareness can significantly impact the dynamics of a relationship. Consider a case where one partner, after recognizing their tendency for codependency, starts setting time aside for personal hobbies and interests, actively cultivating a sense of self outside the relationship. This adjustment shifts the individual's perspective about their needs and worth and can alter how their partner views and treats them. In many instances, as one partner begins to change, the other has a choice: adapt to the new dynamic or continue the old patterns, which no longer find the same foothold.

Addressing and altering one's role in toxic dynamics is not about assigning blame to oneself but about reclaiming power over one's own life and interactions. It's about making conscious choices that affirm your value and contribute to healthier, more balanced relationships. This process of introspection and change is challenging but crucial for anyone trapped in toxic cycles, offering a pathway to healthier relationships and greater personal fulfillment and strength.

1.4 The Science of Attraction: Why We Choose Wrong

Understanding why we are drawn to partners who ultimately bring us pain rather than happiness can be as distressing as the toxic relationships themselves. The roots of our attractions are often deep, tangled in our biological wiring and the societal influences that shape our views on love and relationships. Biologically, our past experiences, especially early life experiences, significantly influence who we find attractive as adults. This is often observed in the phenomenon known as trauma bonding, where the intensity of emotional connection is heightened by experiences of pain, fear, or danger. For instance, if someone has grown up in an environment where affection was intermittently provided alongside abuse, they might subconsciously seek similar patterns in adulthood because it feels familiar. This familiarity, despite being unhealthy, can create a powerful emotional bond that is difficult to break, often mistaking intensity for intimacy.

Moreover, our biological programming can sometimes steer us toward partners who may not be conducive to our well-being. The adrenaline rush of an emotional rollercoaster in a toxic relationship can mimic feelings of passion and excitement, often confused with love. This confusion can be particularly pronounced for those who have experienced past abuse; the body's biochemical reaction to stress and danger—increased adrenaline, cortisol, and dopamine—can be misinterpreted as attraction or love, reinforcing the cycle of trauma bonding.

Societal influences also play a critical role in shaping our perceptions of what is desirable in a partner. Media portrayals often glorify tumultuous relationships, presenting them as passionate and exciting, which can skew our expectations of what love should look like. Films, books, and songs frequently suggest that true love must be hard-won and that obstacles and turmoil are evidence of a deep emotional connection. These portrayals can lead individuals to believe that the highs and lows experienced in toxic relationships are average and even desirable, making it harder for them to recognize authentic, healthy dynamics.

Attachment theory offers a lens through which to view the psychological underpinnings of why we choose partners who may not be suitable for us. This theory suggests that our early attachments—primarily with our caregivers—influence our future relationships. Secure attachments in childhood lead to healthy relationship patterns in adulthood, while insecure attachments can predispose individuals to enter and remain in toxic relationships. Those with anxious attachments may find themselves drawn to partners who validate their fears of abandonment through inconsistent attention. In contrast, those with avoidant attachments might subconsciously choose partners who affirm their belief that intimacy is dangerous or suffocating.

Counteracting these ingrained patterns requires conscious effort and strategies to foster healthier relationships. Mindfulness in dating is one practical approach, encouraging individuals to remain present and critically aware during interactions with potential partners. This practice helps you recognize early warning signs and red flags that might have gone unnoticed or been dismissed. For example, mindfulness can help someone identify if their potential partner exhibits controlling behavior masked as concern or if their intense jealousy is rationalized as passion. Awareness creates a space between feelings and actions, allowing for deliberate, healthier choices rather than reactive ones based on past trauma or societal expectations.

Another preventative strategy is the cultivation of red flag awareness. Educating oneself about the warning signs of toxic behavior can empower individuals to make informed decisions about their relationships. It involves learning about different forms of abuse—emotional, physical, and psychological—and understanding that any form of disrespect, manipulation, or coercion is unacceptable. Workshops, counseling, and extensive reading can equip individuals with the knowledge and tools to recognize and act upon these red flags early in the relationship. This education is crucial for avoiding potentially toxic relationships and building a foundation for healthy, respectful, and loving interactions.

In essence, the science of attraction, when dissected, reveals a complex interplay between our biological predispositions, psychological conditioning, and the societal narratives we consume. By understanding these layers and actively working to navigate our emotional responses and attractions, we are better positioned to choose partners who will enrich our lives and support our well-being, fostering healthy, stable, and fulfilling relationships.

1.5 Common Myths and Misconceptions About Toxic Relationships

One of the most significant barriers to recognizing and addressing toxic relationships is the prevalence of myths and misconceptions that often romanticize or underestimate the seriousness of these interactions. A particularly pervasive myth is the notion that "toxic relationships are just passionate." This idea conflates the intensity of emotional experiences with passion, suggesting that tumultuous relationships are merely a more sincere form of love. However, true passion in relationships fosters growth, respect, and mutual support, not the anxiety, fear, and instability commonly found in toxic dynamics. The belief that intense jealousy or frequent arguments are signs of love can lead individuals to endure harmful situations under the mistaken belief that they are experiencing a deep emotional connection rather than recognizing these signs as indicators of an unhealthy relationship.

Another widespread myth is that one can change a toxic partner. This belief is not only dangerous but also impractical, as it places the responsibility for healing and change on the victim rather than the perpetrator of the toxicity. Change is a deeply personal endeavor and can only be successful when the individual genuinely desires to alter their behavior. Believing that love or persistence can transform a toxic partner often results in cycles of disappointment and further emotional damage as the toxic behaviors continue or escalate. It's crucial to understand that while support can be a powerful catalyst for change, the ultimate responsibility for transformation lies with the individual.

Additionally, there's a common misconception that all toxic relationships involve physical abuse. This misunderstanding overlooks the equally damaging impact of emotional and psychological abuse, which can be more subtle and complex to recognize. Emotional abuse involves tactics like manipulation, gaslighting, and verbal assaults that degrade an individual's self-esteem and independence. Psychological abuse might include isolation, threats, and controlling behaviors that instill fear or dependency. These forms of abuse can leave deep psychological scars, affecting victims' mental health and their ability to form trusting relationships in the future. By educating about these less visible forms of abuse, we can help individuals recognize the signs early and seek help sooner.

The impact of these myths and misconceptions cannot be overstated. They not only perpetuate toxic cycles by normalizing harmful behaviors but also discourage victims from seeking help or exiting the relationship. For instance, if society views frequent, intense arguments as just another form of passion, a person experiencing this may feel that their situation is normal and not seek the help they need. Similarly, the myth that one can change their abusive partner may prevent individuals from leaving harmful situations, perpetuating a cycle of abuse and forgiveness that hinders true healing.

Recognizing and debunking these myths is essential. Education is critical for changing how we perceive and respond to toxic relationships. By providing clear, accurate information about what constitutes a healthy versus a toxic relationship, we can empower individuals to make informed decisions about their interpersonal connections. This involves highlighting the importance of respect, consent, and mutual support in relationships and teaching individuals to recognize the red flags of toxicity. Through workshops, seminars, and accessible literature on the subject, we can begin dismantling the misconceptions that cloud our understanding of healthy relationships, paving the way for more people to seek and cultivate genuinely loving and supportive partnerships.

Understanding these myths and misconceptions is more than an academic exercise; it's a vital step toward empowering ourselves and others to recognize the signs of toxic relationships and to act to protect our well-being. As we challenge these outdated notions, we make room for healthier understandings and practices in love and companionship, encouraging a culture where love is based on mutual respect and joy, not conflict and control.

1.6 The Impact of Social Media on Relationship Perception

In the digital age, social media platforms have become woven into the fabric of our daily lives, influencing how we interact with the world and shaping our perceptions of relationships. Platforms like Instagram, Facebook, and TikTok often present highly curated portrayals of happiness and success, including romantic relationships. These snapshots of perceived perfection are frequently only the highlights of someone's life, meticulously selected to capture the best moments. However, the constant exposure to such idealized images can set unrealistic expectations for our own relationships. We wonder why our daily lives don't measure up to the continuous stream of blissful dates and flawless companionship flooding our feeds. This disparity between reality and social media can skew our understanding of what a healthy relationship should look like, leading us to overlook the natural, less photogenic challenges that all couples face.

Moreover, the pressure to portray one's own relationship as perfect can also be overwhelming. Many individuals feel compelled to post content confirming their happiness and relationship success, which can be particularly misleading during personal doubt or relational strife. This compulsion is driven by the desire for social validation, which, in the context of social media, is often quantified by likes, comments, and shares. In scenarios where relationships are not as stable or happy as they appear online, this pressure can deter individuals from seeking help or even admitting that issues need attention.

The fear of losing the image of a perfect relationship can become a trap, where the appearance on social media becomes more important than the actual health of the relationship itself.

Social media not only influences how we perceive our relationships but can also become an oppressive tool in the hands of a toxic partner. It can be used to manipulate, control, or isolate a person. For instance, a controlling partner might monitor social media interactions closely, dictate what is posted, or even demand passwords. This type of control can isolate the victim from social support networks, making it more difficult for them to reach out for help or even share their real experiences. Manipulation through social media can also manifest in subtler ways, such as a partner persistently undermining one's appearance or decisions in posts or comments, which can erode self-esteem and distort one's sense of self-worth.

However, it's not all doom and gloom. When used wisely, social media can positively affect our relationships. It can keep us connected with friends and family, share significant moments with a broad audience, and even provide platforms for support and advice on relationship issues. The key is cultivating a balanced and healthy approach to social media use. One effective strategy is to evaluate why you are sharing something regularly. Is it to seek validation or genuinely because you want to share a moment? Being honest about your motives can help keep your social media habits healthy and prevent them from negatively impacting your relationships.

Additionally, engaging in regular digital detoxes where you take intentional breaks from social media is beneficial. This helps reduce the influence of unrealistic portrayals on your relationship perceptions and can improve your mental health and well-being. During these breaks, focus on investing in face-to-face interactions and nurturing relationships offline. This strengthens real connections and provides a more balanced perspective on life and relationships, free from the constant need for external validation.

Lastly, critical consumption of content is crucial. Just as we learn to analyze news sources critically, applying similar scrutiny to the relationship content we consume on social media can prevent us from internalizing harmful ideals. Understand that what is posted is often the best version of someone's reality and not an accurate representation of everyday life. By viewing social media content through a critical lens, you can appreciate the positive aspects of these platforms without allowing them to distort your perception of what a healthy relationship looks like.

Navigating social media's impact on relationship perceptions requires awareness, intentional action, and a commitment to online and offline authenticity. By fostering this awareness and taking proactive steps to mitigate the negative influences of social media, we can protect our relationships from unrealistic expectations and maintain a healthier, more grounded view of what it means to love and be loved in the digital age.

TWO

Breaking the Cycle

I f the idea of leaving a toxic relationship feels like stepping into a storm without an umbrella, you're not alone. The complexity and emotional intensity involved can feel daunting, but with the proper preparation and support, you can navigate this storm more safely and effectively. This chapter will equip you with the essential tools and strategies to prepare for your departure from a toxic relationship, ensuring you can do so with the utmost safety and support.

2.1 Preparing to Leave: Safety Plans and Support Systems

When taking the brave step of leaving a toxic relationship, it is crucial to establish a thorough safety plan to ensure your physical and emotional well-being during this critical transition. This plan should involve identifying safe locations to immediately retreat to if needed. Consider contacting trusted friends, family members, or local shelters that provide support and protection to assist you during this challenging time.

Creating a list of emergency contacts is crucial. Compile a comprehensive list including personal contacts familiar with your situation, local emergency services, legal aid, and nearby shelters. It's essential to keep this list in a secure yet easily accessible location or to memorize essential contacts to ensure you can reach out for help when necessary. Also, establish a discreet code word or signal with close friends or family so they can quickly identify when you need urgent assistance without alerting your partner.

In addition, securing your important documents is vital. Gather crucial paperwork such as identification, financial records, legal documents, and personal belongings. Keep these items in a secure location outside your home, such as a safety deposit box or with a trusted confidant, to ensure you have immediate access to them and protect your personal information.

Technology can be an invaluable tool in your safety plan. It's essential to update all your personal devices and accounts with new passwords and privacy settings to prevent unwanted access. Look into discreet communication apps that do not leave a trace of your calls or messages and learn about the emergency features on your smartphone, as they often have quick-access options to contact emergency services without navigating multiple steps.

Interactive Element: Safety Plan Checklist

- Identify safe places to stay temporarily.
- Compile a list of emergency contacts, including personal support and local services.
- Secure important documents and personal items in a safe location.
- Update privacy settings and passwords on all personal devices and accounts.

Creating a robust support system is equally important. Surround yourself with people who understand your situation and are willing to help you through this transition. This network might include close friends, family members, colleagues, or even members of support groups who have had similar experiences. Emotional support is crucial during this time, and logistical support—such as help with moving, temporary housing, or financial assistance—can relieve some of the practical pressures of leaving.

Remember, the decision to leave a toxic relationship is a brave and self-affirming one. While the process can be challenging, having a detailed safety plan and a robust support system can provide you the security and reassurance needed to move forward. You deserve a life free of toxicity, and with the proper preparations, you can start to build a future that reflects your worth and potential.

2.2 Effective Strategies for Ending a Toxic Relationship

When considering ending a toxic relationship, it's crucial to choose the right time and place for this pivotal conversation. Safety is paramount, so it's essential to weigh this decision's emotional and physical implications carefully. Opt for a neutral and public setting that is quiet enough to maintain privacy. This allows for a direct conversation without unnecessary interruptions or distractions. Additionally, consider the timing. It's best to choose a moment when tensions are lower and to avoid times when your partner may be emotionally volatile or under the influence of substances. The goal is to minimize highly charged interactions' emotional and physical risks.

When communicating your decision, it's essential to be direct and unequivocal. Prepare what you intend to say beforehand, and keep your language clear and firm. Focus on using 'I' statements to express your feelings and decisions without blaming or escalating. For example, you might say, "I've decided to end our relationship because I need to feel respected and valued." This approach shifts the conversation to your experience and decision rather than their behavior, which can help reduce defensiveness or an aggressive response. It's also wise to anticipate your partner's reactions and emotionally prepare yourself to stay calm during the conversation.

Be mindful of common emotional traps your partner might use to sway your decision. These can range from promises to change, to threats, or guilt-tripping. It's essential to stay focused on why you are ending the relationship and remember the promises made and not kept. Having a written list of reasons for ending the relationship can serve as a helpful reminder during this challenging conversation.

Following the breakup, prioritizing self-care is essential for managing the stress and emotional upheaval that may follow. Engage in activities that fortify your emotional health and bring you peace, such as spending time with supportive friends or family, participating in physical activities, or seeking solace in nature. Also, consider activities that soothe your spirit and provide comfort, whether reading, listening to music, practicing yoga, or meditating. These practices can help manage immediate stress and build a foundation for your emotional recovery in the future.

The period following the end of a toxic relationship is often marked by a complex mix of emotions—from relief, to grief, or doubt. It's a time when self-care is not just beneficial but necessary. By ensuring that you have strategies to end the relationship safely and to care for yourself afterward, you set the stage for a smoother transition into the next chapter of your life, where respect, self-love, and healthier relationships are the cornerstones. Embrace this phase with kindness towards yourself, allowing time to heal and learn from the past while gradually stepping into a future defined by well-being and inner peace.

2.3 Legal and Financial Considerations When Leaving

In the process of leaving a toxic relationship, dealing with the legal and financial aspects can be overwhelming. However, you must equip yourself with knowledge and take proactive measures to secure your independence and protection. Understanding your legal rights and options is crucial in this process. Depending on your situation, consider legal actions such as obtaining restraining orders for safety, initiating divorce proceedings if married, and arranging for custody of children if applicable. These legal steps are essential for your protection and for establishing boundaries with your former partner. For instance, a restraining order legally requires the individual it is issued against to maintain a certain distance, helping to prevent harassment or abuse post-separation.

Understanding your rights regarding dividing assets, alimony, and other financial settlements is essential, mainly if you have depended financially on your partner. This has a significant impact on your future economic stability. Custody arrangements require careful negotiation and legal scrutiny to ensure the well-being of any children involved. Their emotional and physical safety should be prioritized, and custody decisions should be made in their best interests. Seeking assistance from legal professionals specializing in family law can provide invaluable guidance and representation in navigating these complex issues, ensuring that your rights are protected.

Achieving financial independence is another crucial step after leaving a toxic relationship. Establishing financial autonomy by opening bank accounts in your name and building a credit history can aid in this process. Consulting with financial advisors and accountants can help navigate the complexities of financial separation, including splitting joint accounts, dealing with shared debt, and planning for future financial needs. This professional support is essential for making informed decisions that protect your financial health and provide a stable foundation for your new life.

Documenting everything is also paramount. Keeping meticulous records of all interactions with your former partner, particularly those related to financial transactions or violations of legal boundaries, can be crucial in legal proceedings, especially in contentious situations. Saving copies of relevant communications and financial statements, and documenting incidents of abuse or harassment with dates, times, and the nature of the incidents will provide valuable evidence to support your claims for restraining orders, divorce settlements, or custody arrangements.

During the separation process, surrounding yourself with the right experts and ensuring that all your actions are legally sound and financially prudent is vital to securing your immediate safety and stability. This will lay a solid foundation for a future where you fully control your life and finances. Despite the challenges ahead, proper preparation and professional guidance can help you confidently navigate this phase, paving the way for a life of freedom and peace.

2.4 Dealing with Emotional Backlash Post-Breakup

After you've taken the brave steps to end a toxic relationship, you might find yourself grappling with a rollercoaster of emotions. It's natural to feel everything from relief to intense sadness or anger. Handling these emotions effectively is crucial to your recovery and can prevent you from slipping back into detrimental patterns. The first step is to permit yourself to feel whatever comes up. Suppressing your emotions often leads to them manifesting in other ways, such as physical illness or bursts of uncontrolled anger. Try setting aside specific times during the day to reflect on your feelings. During these sessions, allow yourself to feel without judgment while listening to music that resonates with your mood or writing in a journal.

Journaling can be particularly therapeutic. It allows you to vent frustrations and fears without censorship; over time, it can help you track your healing progress. Writing about your emotions helps in processing them, making them less overwhelming. It provides a private space to confront your feelings, understand them better, and gradually learn to manage them. This practice can be enhanced by focusing on the emotions stemming from the breakup and your hopes and aspirations for the future. This shifts your mental and emotional energy towards recovery and personal growth.

Seeking professional help during this time can be immensely beneficial. Therapists or counselors specializing in post-relationship recovery can offer support and tools tailored to your situation. These professionals can help you understand the dynamics of toxic relationships and the effects they have had on your mental health. They provide a safe space to explore your feelings and offer practical strategies for dealing with them. Therapy can also help in rebuilding your self-esteem and trust in others, which are often damaged in toxic relationships. If face-to-face therapy is not an option, consider online platforms offering flexibility and privacy. Remember, seeking help is a sign of strength and an essential investment in your long-term well-being.

Implementing coping strategies is crucial in managing the stress and emotional upheaval following a breakup. Mindfulness techniques like meditation or focused breathing exercises can help center your thoughts and alleviate anxiety. These practices encourage you to live in the present moment and reduce rumination about past events or future worries, which is common after leaving a toxic relationship. Exercise is another powerful tool. Physical activity releases endorphins, chemicals in your brain that act as natural painkillers and mood elevators. Whether it's a brisk walk in the park, a yoga session, or a more intense workout, find an activity you enjoy and make it a regular part of your routine.

Creative expression is another valuable outlet for your emotions. Engaging in creative activities like painting, writing, or playing music allows you to express feelings that might be hard to articulate verbally. These activities can be compelling in processing complex emotions like grief or betrayal, providing a constructive way to release them. Moreover, creative pursuits can offer a sense of accomplishment and joy, contributing to a more positive self-image and aiding in emotional recovery.

It is also critical to set realistic expectations for your emotional recovery. Healing from a toxic relationship is not linear; it involves ups and downs, and progress might feel slow at times. Understand that some days will be more complicated than others and that setbacks are a normal part of the healing process. It's important not to rush yourself or get discouraged by occasional difficult days. Celebrate small victories, like a day spent without sadness or a moment of genuine laughter. However minor, these signs of progress indicate that you are moving forward. Remember, recovery takes time and patience, but each step you take brings you closer to a life free of toxicity and filled with potential for happiness and peace.

2.5 Handling Mutual Friends and Social Circles

When you decide to leave a toxic relationship, the ripple effects extend beyond just the two people directly involved. Mutual friends and shared social circles often become a complex web of interactions you must navigate carefully. Managing these relationships with tact and mindfulness is essential to protect your emotional well-being and maintain your social support network. One of the first challenges is communicating your side of the story. This isn't about spreading gossip or vilifying your ex-partner but rather about sharing your truth with those who matter to you. When you open up, choose a time and setting that feels comfortable and private. Be honest about your feelings and experiences without delving into unnecessary details or blame. This approach helps maintain your dignity and allows your friends to understand your perspective without feeling coerced into choosing sides.

However, it's crucial to prepare for potential biases. Friends with strong ties to your ex-partner may have conflicting loyalties, and it's essential to approach these situations with an understanding that not everyone may support your decision. In these instances, prioritize your own emotional needs and consider limiting your exposure to any friends who consistently take your ex's side or undermine your feelings. This doesn't necessarily mean ending friendships; instead, you should adjust the level of closeness based on their responses and your comfort level.

Protecting your privacy is another significant concern. Be mindful of the information you share in person and on social media. It's wise to adjust privacy settings on your social media accounts to control who can see your posts, especially if mutual friends are in contact with your ex. Additionally, consider having private conversations with close friends to express your needs and boundaries regarding what information is shared with others. This can include asking them not to relay personal details to your ex or mutual acquaintances. By setting these boundaries, you maintain control over your personal narrative and protect your emotional space.

Rebuilding or strengthening your social connections might seem daunting, especially if the toxic relationship reduces social interactions. Start by contacting old friends you may have lost touch with during your relationship. Rekindle these relationships by sharing positive updates, expressing interest in reconnecting, and planning casual meet-ups. Expanding your social circle by engaging in new activities and hobbies that interest you is also beneficial. This could be anything from joining a book club or fitness class to volunteering for a cause you're passionate about. New activities distract from the emotional turmoil of your breakup and offer opportunities to meet new people who share your interests and can contribute positively to your life.

Deciding who to trust during this period is crucial for your emotional recovery. Evaluate your friendships based on their reactions to your situation and overall behavior. Trustworthy friends listen without judgment, offer support without conditions, and respect your decisions and boundaries. They are the ones who stand by you in difficult times, offering both practical help and emotional comfort. On the other hand, be cautious of friends who dismiss your feelings, push you to "get over it" too quickly, or seem overly interested in the drama of your breakup. Trust your instincts about people's intentions and make conscious choices about whom to confide in.

Navigating your social circles after leaving a toxic relationship requires patience, honesty, and assertiveness. You create a supportive environment that fosters your healing and growth by communicating openly with friends, protecting your privacy, actively rebuilding social connections, and being selective about whom to trust. Remember, true friends respect your journey and offer the support you need to move forward into a healthier, happier chapter of your life.

2.6 No Contact Rule: Importance and Execution

Initiating and maintaining no contact with a toxic ex-partner can profoundly impact your emotional and psychological healing process. This strategy isn't merely about cutting off communication; it's about reclaiming your peace and allowing yourself the space to heal without interference. The psychological benefits are substantial: by removing the constant triggers and potential manipulations that come with ongoing contact, you allow your stress levels to decrease thereby letting yourself to break the cycle of dependency and emotional turmoil often sustained in toxic relationships. Essentially, no contact acts as a boundary that protects your emotional landscape, enabling you to regain strength and perspective that was likely compromised during the relationship.

Implementing a no-contact rule effectively requires a clear, resolute decision and a strategic plan to maintain it. Start by communicating your decision to the other party in a straightforward, non-confrontational manner, ensuring you articulate that this measure is necessary for your personal healing. After clarifying your intentions, take practical steps such as blocking their number on your phone, email, and all social media accounts. This reduces the temptation to check in on them and helps avoid any messages that might pull you back into emotional turmoil. If you share mutual friends or professional connections, set clear boundaries about what information, if any, you are comfortable being shared with your ex.

It's essential to handle any attempts from your ex-partner to violate the no-contact rule. They may contact you through various platforms or mutual connections. Staying firm and reminding yourself why you established this rule is crucial. If they do reach out to you, it's best to refrain from responding. Consider keeping a record of the attempt, especially if it is necessary for legal reasons later. If you have shared responsibilities like co-parenting, aim for minimal contact and strictly business-like communication methods. Keep the conversations focused on the matter at hand and avoid personal topics.

Dealing with urges to reconnect can be one of the most challenging aspects of maintaining no contact, especially during moments of loneliness or vulnerability. It is essential to have strategies in place for these moments. Redirect your focus by engaging in healthier activities that fulfill your emotional needs, such as spending time with supportive friends or family, diving into a new hobby, or allowing yourself some quiet time to read or walk. Keeping a journal can also be helpful; write down your feelings instead of acting impulsively to reach out. This helps you process your emotions safely and reminds you why you chose to implement no contact in the first place.

Legal and safety considerations are also important, mainly if you're dealing with a situation with implications for shared assets, custody, or a threat of violence. In such cases, consulting with a legal professional to understand your rights and formalize the no-contact rule through a restraining order or similar legal measures is advisable. This is especially critical if children are involved or your financial entanglements require negotiation and settlement. Such legal backing adds a layer of safety and a strong deterrent against any attempts to violate established boundaries.

By effectively implementing the no-contact rule, you protect your emotional health and fortify your journey toward a life free from toxicity. This rule isn't just about avoiding the other person; it's about creating the environment for profound personal growth and healing.

As this chapter concludes, remember that breaking the cycle of a toxic relationship is a process that involves recognizing the need for change, preparing strategically for this change, and implementing steps that safeguard your emotional and physical well-being. The no-contact rule is a crucial strategy in this process, serving as a protective boundary that fosters healing and empowerment. Moving forward, the insights and strategies outlined here will guide you as you navigate the initial and often turbulent phase of post-breakup recovery, setting the foundation for healthier, more fulfilling relationships in the future.

THREE

Healing from Emotional Trauma

W hen the shadows of a toxic relationship finally lift, the light
that floods in might reveal the deep emotional injuries left
behind. Healing from these wounds requires more than time; it
requires dedicated effort and understanding. You may find yourself
haunted by memories of past hurts or gripped by fear without a clear
cause. These experiences can be symptomatic of Post-Traumatic
Stress Disorder (PTSD), a condition that, though commonly associated with war veterans, is also prevalent among those who have
survived intense toxic relationships. This chapter will guide you
through recognizing the signs of PTSD, identifying triggers, and
employing strategies to manage your symptoms, setting you on a
path to regain control over your emotional health.

3.1 Understanding and Managing PTSD After Toxic Relationships

Identifying Symptoms of PTSD

Post-Traumatic Stress Disorder (PTSD) can be a debilitating condition that emerges after experiencing severe emotional trauma, including the trauma stemming from toxic relationships. Symptoms of PTSD vary widely, but they typically include flashbacks, where you vividly re-experience moments of trauma; nightmares that disrupt your sleep; severe anxiety that doesn't seem to subside; and uncontrollable thoughts about the relationship. You might find yourself persistently sad or numb, detached from people and activities that once brought you joy. Alternatively, you might feel hyper alert, always looking for danger, or excessively startled by ordinary things. Recognizing these symptoms is the first critical step toward healing. It's important to understand that these reactions are not signs of weakness but rather normal responses to abnormal emotional injuries you endured.

Explaining the Triggers

Triggers are specific reminders of past trauma that can cause your PTSD symptoms to flare up. These triggers can be as obvious as visiting a place you associate with your toxic relationship or as subtle as a scent or a sound that unconsciously reminds you of a distressing event. Even certain conversations or emotional states that mirror those experienced during the toxic relationship can serve as triggers. Recognizing these triggers is essential for managing your PTSD. It involves a process of self-reflection and, often, help from a therapist to identify patterns in your responses to certain stimuli. By understanding what triggers your PTSD symptoms, you can begin to develop strategies to either avoid these triggers or to cope with them more effectively when they cannot be avoided.

Techniques to Manage Symptoms

Managing PTSD symptoms can be challenging, but several effective techniques can offer relief. Grounding exercises help you regain your sense of reality during or following a flashback or panic attack. These might include tactile exercises, like holding a piece of ice, to focus your senses away from the flashback and back to the present. Controlled breathing exercises also play a crucial role in managing anxiety. Techniques such as diaphragmatic breathing, where you focus on making your stomach rise and fall with each breath, can help calm your nervous system and reduce the intensity of your anxiety. Creating a safe mental environment is another crucial strategy. This involves cultivating a physical or psychological space where you can retreat to feel safe and secure. This space could be a room in your home that promotes relaxation and comfort or a mental visualization of a tranquil setting where you feel safe.

When to Seek Professional Help

While self-help techniques can be very effective, there are times when professional help is necessary. If your symptoms persist, worsen, or significantly interfere with your daily activities and quality of life, it is crucial to seek professional psychological help. Therapists specialized in trauma can provide support and therapy modalities that address the roots of your PTSD. Finding the right therapist is vital. Look for professionals with trauma experience who make you feel safe and understood. Many therapists offer a consultation session, which can be an excellent opportunity to see if their approach suits your needs. Don't hesitate to seek help; professional therapists can offer new insights into your experiences and provide tools to manage your symptoms effectively.

Interactive Element: PTSD Symptom Checklist

- Flashbacks: Experiencing vivid, intrusive memories of traumatic events.
- Severe Anxiety: Persistent, excessive worry that does not subside.
- Nightmares: Frequent distressing dreams related to traumatic events.
- Emotional Numbness: Feeling detached from emotions and surroundings.
- Hyperarousal: Being easily startled or constantly on edge.

Use this checklist to identify any symptoms you might be experiencing. Recognizing these signs is the first step towards managing PTSD and moving forward in your healing process.

In essence, understanding and managing PTSD requires a multi-faceted approach that includes recognizing symptoms, identifying triggers, employing practical management techniques, and knowing when to seek professional help. By addressing each of these aspects, you can begin to loosen the grip of PTSD on your life, reclaiming your emotional independence and moving towards a happier, healthier future.

3.2 Therapeutic Approaches for Emotional Recovery

The path to emotional recovery after a toxic relationship can often feel like navigating a labyrinth—complex and confusing. Fortunately, various therapeutic approaches have been developed to guide you through this maze, each offering unique benefits and strategies.

Cognitive-behavioral therapy (CBT), dialectical behavior therapy (DBT), and eye movement desensitization and reprocessing (EMDR) are among the most effective treatments for those emerging from toxic relationships. Understanding these options can empower you to choose which therapeutic path best suits your needs and circumstances.

CBT is a widely recognized approach that identifies and changes negative thought patterns and behaviors. It operates on the principle that our thoughts, feelings, and behaviors are interconnected and that we can influence others by changing one. For survivors of toxic relationships, CBT can be particularly effective in addressing persistent negative self-beliefs—such as feelings of worthlessness or inadequacy—that these relationships often instill. By working with a therapist to identify these harmful patterns, you can replace them with more positive and constructive thoughts, leading to healthier behaviors and emotional outcomes.

DBT, another transformative therapy, was initially developed to treat borderline personality disorder but has since been found to be immensely helpful for a range of issues, including those stemming from emotional abuse. Its focus is teaching skills to cope with stress, regulate emotions, and improve relationships. Core to DBT is the concept of mindfulness, or being fully present at the moment, which can help you become more aware of and responsive to your emotional states rather than being overwhelmed by them. DBT also emphasizes developing distress tolerance skills—crucial for anyone in a volatile relationship—and interpersonal effectiveness, which can empower you to set and maintain healthy boundaries.

EMDR is somewhat different in its approach but no less impactful. This therapy is specifically designed to help people process and recover from trauma. It involves recalling distressing images while receiving one of several types of bilateral sensory input, such as side-to-side eye movements or hand tapping. EMDR works by helping the brain reprocess the traumatic memories so that they no longer trigger intense emotional responses. This can be particularly beneficial if you find yourself haunted by specific memories of your toxic relationship that trigger fear, anxiety, or sadness.

Integrating these therapies into your daily life extends the benefits beyond your sessions. For instance, the cognitive restructuring skills learned in CBT can be practiced anytime you notice negative thoughts creeping in. Similarly, the mindfulness techniques central to DBT can be employed daily to help maintain emotional balance, whether at work, interacting with friends, or spending time alone. EMDR might not lend itself as readily to daily integration, but understanding the process can help you manage moments when memories become overwhelming, grounding you more firmly in the present.

The effectiveness of these therapies is not just theoretical. Consider the story of "Anna," who entered therapy after ending a profoundly toxic relationship that had left her doubting her worth and struggling with anxiety. Through CBT, Anna worked to identify and challenge the pervasive negative thoughts she had about herself, gradually replacing them with affirmations of her value and strengths. Meanwhile, DBT helped her develop tools to manage her anxiety and communicate more effectively with those around her, reinforcing her recovery. Anna's journey through therapy brought her not just relief from her immediate suffering but a new, more positive outlook on life—a testament to the power of targeted therapeutic intervention.

Choosing the right therapy can be a transformative part of your healing process, providing the tools to recover and thrive. Whether it's the thought pattern transformation offered by CBT, the emotional regulation skills of DBT, or the trauma processing power of EMDR, each therapeutic approach provides a unique pathway out of the aftermath of toxic relationships and into a brighter, more stable future. As you consider these options, remember that the most crucial step is reaching out for help, setting you firmly on the path to recovery.

3.3 The Role of Mindfulness and Meditation in Healing

Mindfulness and meditation are often mentioned in the same breath, but they hold unique places in the practice of mental and emotional healing. Mindfulness is the quality of being fully present and engaged in the moment, aware of your thoughts and feelings without distraction or judgment. Meditation, conversely, is the practice of focusing your mind in silence to increase awareness of the present moment, which often incorporates mindfulness techniques. While general relaxation techniques like taking a hot bath or listening to soothing music are designed to relieve stress, mindfulness and medi-tation temporarily delve deeper, transforming how you relate to experiences, particularly stress and anxiety.

One of the profound benefits of mindfulness and meditation in the healing process is their ability to reduce stress. This is achieved by lowering physiological stress responses, such as heart rate and blood pressure, and by reducing cortisol levels, a hormone associated with stress. Moreover, these practices improve emotional reaction control, training you to observe your feelings and thoughts without becoming overwhelmed or reactive. This is particularly invaluable when recovering from emotional trauma, where feelings of anger, sadness, or fear can be intense and unpredictable. Through regular mindfulness and meditation, you can develop a steadier emotional state, fostering a greater sense of peace and stability in your life.

Guided mindfulness exercises and meditation routines can be benefi-cial for individuals recovering from emotional trauma. For example, a simple mindfulness exercise involves focusing on your breath. Sit comfortably, close your eyes, and take slow, deep breaths. Concentrate on the sensation of air entering and leaving your body, and if your mind wanders, gently bring your focus back to your breath. This exercise helps anchor you in the present moment, providing a break from distressing memories or worries about the future. For meditation, a guided imagery routine can be effective. Visualize a peaceful place, perhaps a quiet beach or a serene forest. Imagine yourself there, exploring the environment with all your senses. This practice provides a mental escape from stress and enhances your ability to concentrate and relax.

Developing a consistent practice of mindfulness and meditation can offer long-term benefits that go beyond immediate stress relief. Regular practice can alter the brain's neuroplasticity, leading to improved regulation of emotions and increased mental flexibility. Over time, this can lead to enduring changes in how you experience and respond to stress, making you more resilient to future challenges. To incorporate mindfulness into your daily routine, consider setting aside a specific time each day for practice. It could be a few minutes before starting your day or in the evening before bed. The key is consistency, as the benefits of mindfulness and meditation build over time.

Furthermore, mindfulness can be integrated into everyday activities to enhance its benefits. For instance, practice mindful eating by paying close attention to your food's taste, texture, and sensations. This can turn a daily activity into a mindfulness practice, helping you stay anchored in the present throughout the day. Similarly, engage in mindful walking by focusing on the sensation of your feet touching the ground, the sounds around you, or the feeling of the air on your skin. These practices relieve stress and deepen your connection to the present moment, enriching your daily life with a heightened awareness and appreciation.

By embracing mindfulness and meditation, you equip yourself with powerful tools to navigate the healing process, transforming how you relate to your thoughts, emotions, and experiences. These practices offer a pathway to recovery that fosters a profound sense of peace and resilience, enabling you to move forward from past trauma with grace and strength.

3.4 Rebuilding Self-Esteem and Self-Worth

After exiting the tumultuous waves of a toxic relationship, you might find your sense of self-worth has taken a significant hit. It's not uncommon to emerge feeling diminished, your self-esteem eroded by the relentless negativity or manipulation you endured. The journey to rebuild this integral part of your psyche involves deep introspection and a series of deliberate actions. Initially, assessing the damage done to your self-esteem is crucial. This process consists of reflecting on how you view yourself now versus before the relationship. Ask yourself: Do you feel less confident? Are there specific areas in your life where you feel inadequate? Perhaps you doubt your decision-making skills or feel unworthy of happiness and success. Identifying these areas provides a clear starting point for rebuilding your self-esteem.

Engaging in positive self-affirmations can be a transformative tool in this healing process. Affirmations are positive, empowering statements that, when spoken repeatedly, can help to reshape your subconscious thoughts, shifting them from negative to positive. For instance, replacing thoughts of unworthiness with affirmations like, "I am deserving of respect and love," can gradually alter your internal dialogue. These affirmations must resonate with you so they genuinely feel empowering. You might start by writing down qualities you genuinely like about yourself or achievements you are proud of, then turn these into daily affirmations. Reciting these affirmations each morning, or whenever doubt creeps in, can be a powerful reminder of your intrinsic worth.

Moreover, engaging in activities that boost self-esteem can accelerate your path to recovery. Goal setting is particularly effective. Setting and achieving small, manageable goals can restore faith in your abilities. These goals don't have to be monumental; they can be as simple as cooking a new recipe, finishing a book, or completing a small project at work. Success in these endeavors creates a positive feedback loop in your brain, boosting your confidence with each accomplishment. Success journaling, where you record every success, no matter how small, can further reinforce this positive self-perception. Each entry is tangible proof of your capabilities and progress, which can be incredibly uplifting during moments of doubt.

Celebrating small wins is another crucial step in rebuilding self-esteem. This practice helps shift your focus from what you perceive as failures to recognizing and appreciating your progress. Did you express your feelings in a situation where you usually stay silent? Celebrate that. Were you able to set a boundary and stick to it? That's another win. Acknowledging these small victories helps build a sense of self-efficacy and pride. Over time, this rebuilds damaged self-esteem and encourages a more positive outlook.

Incorporating these strategies into your daily life doesn't just patch up the wounds left by a toxic relationship; it strengthens your overall emotional resilience, equipping you to face future challenges with a robust sense of self-worth. As you apply these practices, you'll notice a gradual but unmistakable shift in how you view yourself and your place in the world. This renewed self-esteem, built on self-compassion and acknowledgment, will protect you from future relational harms and empower you to pursue your life's goals confidently and clearly.

3.5 Forgiveness: Is It Necessary and How to Achieve It?

Forgiveness in the context of recovering from a toxic relationship can often feel like an impossible challenge. You might ask, "Why should I forgive someone who has hurt me so deeply?" This is a valid question that underscores forgiveness's complex nature. Understanding forgiveness as a process that primarily benefits you rather than the offender is crucial. It's not about condoning the hurtful actions or dismissing your pain; it's about freeing yourself from the lingering anger and resentment that can tether you to the past. Forgiveness can be a decisive step towards healing, allowing you to reclaim your emotional energy and focus on building a positive future. However, it's also important to recognize that forgiveness is a personal choice and requires sincere readiness and effort.

The benefits of forgiveness extend beyond emotional relief. It can reduce stress, lower the risk of depression, and increase feelings of optimism, all of which can enhance overall well-being. Yet, the path to forgiveness is often fraught with challenges. The process can stir up emotions you may have felt were resolved or diminished. You might experience a resurgence of anger or sadness as you confront the pain that was inflicted upon you. Additionally, there can be a significant internal conflict between the part of you that wants to hold on to the hurt as a form of emotional protection and the part that wants to let go and move forward. Recognizing these challenges is the first step in navigating them effectively.

If direct forgiveness feels too difficult, there are alternative approaches to consider that can also facilitate emotional healing. Acceptance, for example, can be a viable path when forgiveness seems unattainable. This involves acknowledging what happened and accepting that it cannot be changed. Acceptance doesn't mean agreeing with or liking what occurred, but it does mean no longer resisting the reality of the past. It allows you to lessen the emotional hold on your present life, providing a way to move forward without the explicit need to forgive.

For those who choose to pursue forgiveness, breaking the process into manageable steps can be helpful. Begin by clearly acknowledging the hurt that you've experienced. Recognize how it has affected you both emotionally and physically. Allowing yourself to feel the full impact of your pain is often painful but necessary for genuine healing. Next, consider the context of the relationship and the circumstances that might have influenced the other person's behavior. This is not about excusing their actions but understanding them in a broader context, which can sometimes make forgiveness more achievable.

Continuing through the forgiveness process, gradually work towards releasing your anger and resentment. This might involve expressing your emotions through writing, speaking to a therapist, or even talking directly to the person who hurt you if it's safe and appropriate. Each small step in expressing and releasing these feelings can significantly reduce their power over you. Finally, actively choose to let go of the grievance. This often requires a conscious decision not to let the hurt define you or your future relationships. It might involve rituals of letting go, like writing down your feelings and burning the paper, or simply setting a daily intention to live free from bitterness.

Throughout this process, be patient with yourself. Forgiveness is rarely linear, and it's expected to move back and forth between feelings of anger and acceptance. Each step forward, no matter how small, is progress towards reclaiming your emotional freedom and opening your heart to the potential of a healthier, happier life free from the shadows of past hurts. As you navigate this path, remember that forgiveness, at its core, is a gift you give to yourself, a vital act of self-compassion that can brighten the darkest of past experiences and lead you toward a more fulfilling future.

3.6 The Power of Emotional Detox: Techniques to Cleanse Your Mind

After the storm of a toxic relationship has passed, it's common to find residual negativity clinging to your thoughts and emotions. These remnants, which I call emotional toxins, can continue to cloud your mind and spirit, hindering your ability to move forward and embrace a healthier, happier life. Recognizing these toxins is the first step in undertaking an emotional detox—a process as critical to your mental health as physical detoxing is to your body. Emotional toxins can manifest as persistent feelings of anger, resentment, sadness, or fear—emotions that once served as your psychological armor against the hurt inflicted by others.

To embark on an emotional detox, consider the cathartic power of writing letters you never intend to send. This exercise lets you express your feelings and thoughts towards your former partner or the relationship. Pour everything into these letters—your anger, disappointment, sorrow, and regrets. Writing without the filter of politeness or the pressure of confrontation can be incredibly liberating. Once written, you might destroy these letters as a symbolic gesture of letting go or keep them as a reminder of the emotional journey you've traversed.

Creative expression is another potent detox technique. Engage in activities like painting, sculpting, writing poetry, or composing music —any creative work that resonates with you. These activities aren't just outlets for your emotions but also ways to translate your feelings into something beautiful and meaningful, transforming pain into art. The creation process is inherently therapeutic and can provide profound insights into your feelings and how your experiences have shaped them.

Therapeutic rituals can also play a crucial role in your emotional detox. These might include 'letting go' ceremonies where you physically release something that represents your past pain. For example, you could write down hurtful memories on paper and then burn them or throw stones into a body of water, each representing a toxic memory you wish to release. By giving physical expression to emotional release, these rituals can help solidify your intentions to move forward and cleanse your mind of toxic residues.

Incorporating routine emotional check-ins is like maintaining a garden; it prevents weeds from taking over and ensures that new, healthy growth has the space to flourish. Set aside regular times— perhaps weekly or biweekly—to reflect on your emotional state. Ask yourself what feelings occupy the most room in your mind and whether they serve your well-being. This ongoing self-assessment helps prevent the buildup of negative emotions and ensures that issues are addressed before they grow too large. It's a practice that fosters more profound self-awareness and control over your emotional health.

Maintaining a clean emotional slate moving forward requires consistent effort. Implement regular self-care routines that nourish and rejuvenate your spirit. This might include daily practices such as meditation, exercise, or engaging in hobbies that bring you joy and relaxation. The key is to create a lifestyle that supports emotional cleanliness and robust health. Regularly investing in activities that uplift and support you reinforces your emotional resilience and reduces the likelihood of old toxins reclaiming territory in your mind.

When applied diligently and thoughtfully, these techniques can help you purge the emotional toxins left by toxic relationships. They offer a pathway to a clearer, more peaceful mind, where the shadows of the past no longer loom over your present happiness.

As this chapter closes, the tools and insights shared here are not just about recovery; they're about empowering you to lead a life defined not by what you've endured but by what you aspire to achieve. The journey of healing is personal and universal—no one's path is exactly the same, but the landmarks of understanding, coping, and eventually thriving are common to all. As we turn the page to the next chapter, we carry forward the lessons of resilience and renewal, ready to explore deeper into personal growth and relationship building.

FOUR

Rediscovering Self-Love and Respect

Have you ever paused amid your daily hustle, feeling like you're merely existing rather than thriving? We often realize our well-being has taken a backseat in these quiet moments. As you move beyond toxic relationships, it becomes crucial to redirect your focus inward and prioritize self-care. This isn't about indulgence—crafting a lifestyle where self-love and respect are at the forefront, guiding you toward a more fulfilled and balanced existence. In this chapter, we delve into nurturing your well-being through a tailored self-care regimen that respects your unique life circumstances and evolves with you.

4.1 Designing Your Self-Care Regimen

Understand Self-Care Needs

Self-care is often pictured as a one-size-fits-all package of spa days and meditation. However, effective self-care is profoundly personal and varies widely depending on individual needs. It encompasses physical, emotional, and mental aspects, each requiring attention and understanding. Start by assessing your current state in these areas. Physically, are you getting enough rest, nutrition, and exercise? Emotionally, do you feel stable and supported, or are there unresolved issues weighing you down? Mentally, consider your stress levels and general outlook on life. Identifying these needs is the first step in creating a self-care plan that nurtures you.

Create a Personalized Self-Care Plan

With a clear understanding of your needs, you can craft a self-care plan that effectively addresses each aspect. Incorporate elements like regular physical activity that boosts your health and mood. Tailor your diet to what energizes and nourishes your body. Prioritize sleep, ensuring a restful environment and a routine that promotes quality rest. For emotional care, engage in activities that reduce stress and bring joy, such as connecting with loved ones or pursuing hobbies. Lastly, include mental health practices like journaling or therapy to maintain your psychological well-being.

Implementing the Plan

Incorporating your self-care regimen into your daily routine can be challenging, especially when faced with time constraints and fluctuating motivation. To navigate this, start small. Integrate activities into your schedule gradually, and set realistic goals. For instance, begin with a 10-minute meditation each morning rather than a full hour. Use tools like apps to remind and motivate you, and perhaps most importantly, treat each act of self-care as an appointment with yourself—a non-negotiable part of your day.

Evaluating and Adjusting the Plan

Self-care is not a static practice; it requires flexibility to adapt as your life and needs evolve. Regularly review your self-care plan—perhaps every month or with each season—to assess what's working and what isn't. Are you feeling more energized and balanced, or are some areas still lacking? Adjust your strategies, perhaps by trying new activities or tweaking your routine. This ongoing process ensures that your self-care regimen remains effective and responsive to your needs, supporting your journey toward lasting self-love and respect.

Embarking on this path of tailored self-care enhances your quality of life and empowers you to stand more robustly against life's challenges. By committing to self-care, you affirm your worth and take active steps towards a happier, healthier you.

4.2 Setting and Respecting Personal Boundaries

Within the gardens of our personal space, boundaries are the fences that keep us safe and respected; they define where we end and others begin. Recognizing the areas where boundaries are necessary is the first step toward cultivating a healthy environment for yourself. These areas often span the emotional, where you need to protect your feelings from being disregarded; the physical, safeguarding your personal space; and the digital, which involves managing your interactions on social media and other online platforms. Each space requires clear boundaries to ensure your relationships are respectful and nurturing rather than draining and disruptive.

To establish these boundaries, identify what feels non-negotiable to you in these areas. For instance, you might decide that you need to have time alone to decompress after work, that your phone is off-limits to everyone but you, or that you will not tolerate belittling comments in any form. Once you've identified these needs, the next step is communicating them to those around you. This can be challenging, especially if you're not used to asserting yourself, but it's crucial for maintaining your well-being. Use "I" statements to express your needs assertively and respectfully, such as, "I need some quiet time when I get home. I'd appreciate it if we could save any discussions after dinner." This approach focuses on your needs and feelings rather than sounding accusatory.

However, even the most explicit boundaries can be tested or violated. When this happens, it is essential to respond promptly and firmly. Reaffirm your boundaries by restating them and explaining the impact of the violation. For example, if someone interrupts your alone time, you might say, "As I mentioned, I need this hour to myself. When you interrupt, it makes it hard for me to recharge. I need you to respect this time, as it's important for my well-being." If violations persist, consider implementing consequences, which might involve limiting your availability to the person or withdrawing from interactions that consistently disrespect your boundaries.

Remember, setting and enforcing boundaries is not just about keeping others at bay; it's a profound act of self-respect. It communicates to yourself and others that your feelings, body, and time are valuable and worthy of respect. This boosts your self-esteem and improves the quality of your relationships. People learn how to treat us based on what we accept from them. By setting clear boundaries, you teach those around you how you expect to be treated— with consideration and respect. This establishes a positive dynamic where your needs are acknowledged and met, allowing relationships to flourish on a foundation of mutual respect and understanding.

You'll likely discover a newfound sense of empowerment as you set and enforce these boundaries. Each act of boundary-setting is a step towards a more respected, more authentic self. It's a journey that enhances your interactions with others and your relationship with yourself, reinforcing a cycle of respect and self-care that propels you toward fulfillment and peace.

4.3 Overcoming the Fear of Loneliness: The Joy of Being Alone

Often, the silence of solitude is mistakenly filled with the echoes of loneliness, casting a shadow over the opportunity to discover the peace and joy inherent in spending time alone. It's crucial to shift this perception and to start viewing solitude not as a sign of isolation but as a valuable space for self-reflection and personal growth. When you change how you perceive being alone, you transform it from a state of lack to a state of abundance—an abundance of time, space, and freedom to explore your own deepest needs and desires without distraction.

Redefining alone time begins with recognizing its value. Think of it as a personal retreat, a chance to return to your center and recharge in ways that crowded, noisy environments and demanding schedules don't permit. In these quiet moments, you're not answering to anyone; you're free to simply be. It's a time when you can fully engage with your thoughts, listen to your inner voice, and make decisions that align with your self-interest. This redefinition helps shift the emotional response to solitude from one of anxiety or fear to one of anticipation and openness.

Embracing solitude also opens up a world where you can enjoy activities just for the pleasures they bring you, without the need to accommodate anyone else's preferences or schedules. Consider the simple joy of uninterrupted time reading a book, taking a long walk in nature, or engaging in a hobby you love. These activities bring satisfaction and enhance your self-reliance as you learn to be your own source of entertainment and happiness. Cooking a meal for one, for example, can be an act of self-love, where you get to indulge in preparing and eating foods that you genuinely enjoy without compromise—or perhaps, engaging in solo sports like swimming or cycling, where the rhythm of your activity allows you to fall into a meditative state, clearing your mind and strengthening your body simultaneously.

The journey towards enjoying your own company can be complicated and might require a gradual approach, especially if being alone triggers feelings of unease. Start by setting aside short periods to be alone, doing something you genuinely enjoy. Gradually increase this time as your comfort level grows. This practice helps build confidence in being alone, showing you that solitude can be enjoyable and enriching rather than something to be feared. Additionally, use this time to practice mindfulness, focusing on the present moment and the activity rather than letting your mind wander to feelings of loneliness or isolation.

The benefits of spending time alone extend beyond mere enjoyment. Solitude offers significant psychological and emotional advantages, such as increased creativity. When you're alone, your mind can wander more freely, exploring ideas and solutions without interruption. This can lead to greater creativity as you connect thoughts and concepts in novel ways, unrestricted by the input or criticism of others. Better self-awareness is another profound benefit. Alone time forces you to confront your true feelings and thoughts, which can lead to greater self-understanding and clarity about your life and your goals. Furthermore, solitude can be incredibly restorative. In a world constantly buzzing with activity and noise, having the space to step back and breathe can help reduce stress and mental fatigue, resetting your emotional compass.

Learning to appreciate and embrace your time alone will enrich your life unexpectedly. It will provide depth and balance to your social interactions and help you understand your relationships even more. By cultivating a positive and proactive approach to solitude, you conquer the fear of loneliness and open the door to a more self-aware, creative, and emotionally resilient version of yourself.

4.4 Reclaiming Your Identity Beyond Relationships

In the wake of a relationship, especially a toxic one, it's not uncommon to feel as though a part of you has been lost or overshadowed by the experiences you've endured. This is why rediscovering and reaffirming who you are outside of any relationship is beneficial and necessary. It's about peeling back the layers of influence—good and bad—that relationships have imprinted upon you and returning to the core of what makes you uniquely you. Let's begin by identifying your values and interests. These aspects resonate deeply with you, the non-negotiables that define your character and guide your decisions. When you felt most fulfilled or proud of yourself—what values were you upholding? Was it honesty, creativity, independence, or perhaps compassion?

Similarly, reflect on activities that ignite your passion or bring you peace. It could be anything from painting and hiking to volunteering and writing. Understanding these can help you align your life closely with what truly brings you joy and fulfillment.

Once you understand your values and interests, the next step is to craft a vision for your future. This vision should reflect your true self, uninfluenced by past partners or the expectations of others. It's about envisioning a life that feels authentic and fulfilling to you. Start by setting some time aside for quiet reflection or meditation. Visualize where you see yourself in the next few years, not just in your career or achievements but, more importantly, in your personal growth and relationships. What kind of activities are you doing? Who are you surrounded by? What values are you living by? This vision can serve as a guiding light, helping to steer you back on track whenever you feel lost or swayed by external influences.

With this vision in place, setting personal goals becomes the vehicle for making your vision a reality. These goals should be specific, measurable, achievable, relevant, and time-bound—SMART, as often referred to. More importantly, they should align with your vision and values. For instance, if one of your core values is health and your vision includes a fit and active lifestyle, a goal might be to run a half marathon within the year. Or, if creativity is central to your identity, perhaps your goal is to complete a novel or showcase your art in a local exhibition. The key is to ensure these goals resonate with your aspirations and are steps toward the life you envision for yourself.

Celebrating your achievements is crucial in reinforcing your sense of identity. Every goal met, every project completed, and every challenge overcome is a testament to your capabilities and a building block of your self-esteem. Make it a habit to acknowledge these achievements, no matter how small. Keep a success journal, or take a moment to reflect on and savor your success. This practice boosts your mood and motivation and solidifies your sense of self. It's a reminder that you are capable and worthy and that your actions are powerful and meaningful.

As you embark on this journey of self-discovery and personal development, remember that each step, each choice, and each day is a part of crafting a life that feels as authentic and vibrant as possible. Through understanding your fundamental values and interests, crafting a vision for your life, pursuing meaningful goals, and celebrating your victories, you gradually build a life that genuinely reflects who you are, independent of anyone else's influence or expectations. This is the essence of reclaiming your identity—a powerful affirmation of your individuality and a celebration of your resilience and strength.

4.5 Cultivating Positive Self-Talk and Thought Patterns

The words we whisper to ourselves have more power than one might imagine, shaping our self-image and influencing our emotional well-being. Recognizing negative self-talk is the initial step towards transforming how you relate to yourself, especially if your inner narrative has been tainted by past toxic relationships. These relationships may have planted seeds of doubt, unworthiness, or failure, which can grow into persistent, harmful dialogues that replay in your mind. To start changing this narrative, become an observer of your thoughts. Pay attention to the occasions when you put yourself down or question your worth. Are these thoughts factual, or are they distortions of the truth? Identifying these moments is crucial, as they offer the opportunity to challenge and change the narrative.

Once you've pinpointed negative self-talk patterns, the next phase is to actively dispute and replace these thoughts with positive and self-affirming ones. This process, often called cognitive restructuring, involves questioning the validity of negative thoughts and reframing them to promote a more positive and realistic perspective. For example, if you think, "I always fail in everything I do," challenge this by recalling instances where you have succeeded. Then, reshape the thought to something more balanced, such as, "Sometimes I face challenges, but I also have many successes." This practice negates the negative and reinforces the recognition of your capabilities and worth.

Practicing daily affirmations can further reinforce this new, positive self-dialogue. Affirmations are positive statements about yourself that, when repeated often, can help to cement a more positive view of your self-worth. Start by writing a list of affirmations that resonate with you, such as "I am competent," "I am worthy of respect," or "I am a loving and caring person." Integrate these affirmations into your daily routine by saying them out loud every morning, writing them in a journal, or even posting them around your home where you'll see them regularly. Over time, these affirmations can help overwrite the old, negative beliefs reinforced by toxic interactions, fostering a healthier and more positive self-image.

Mindfulness, the practice of being fully present and engaged, can effectively manage negative thoughts and emotions. It teaches you to observe your thoughts and feelings without judgment, recognizing that they are transient and do not define you. This can be remarkably liberating if you're struggling with recurring negative thoughts. Practicing mindfulness teaches you to detach from these thoughts, viewing them as passing mental events rather than truths about who you are. Simple mindfulness exercises, like focusing on your breath or engaging all your senses when activity performing a routine, can help anchor you in the present moment, reducing the impact and frequency of negative thoughts.

This integration of mindfulness assists in handling momentary negative thoughts and contributes to a longer-term shift in how you perceive and react to mental and emotional challenges. Adopting a more mindful approach to your thoughts and emotions fosters resilience, allowing you to face stress and negativity with a calmer, more balanced perspective. This enhances your emotional well-being and empowers you to navigate the complexities of life with a stronger, more grounded sense of self.

As you continue to practice these strategies, you will likely notice a shift in how you talk to yourself and how you feel about yourself. Replacing negative self-talk with positive affirmations and mindfulness transforms your internal dialogue, which increases self-esteem and confidence. This change is profound, affecting every aspect of your life, from how you handle stress and relate to others to how you pursue your goals and dreams. It's a testament to the power of words and thoughts and a reminder that you can truly change your life by changing these.

4.6 Harnessing Creativity for Emotional Expression

Creativity isn't just an avenue for artistic expression or an idle pastime—it's a profound therapeutic tool that offers a unique way for individuals to process and express complex emotions. When you channel your feelings into creative activities, you transform intangible emotions into something tangible, which can be incredibly liberating. Engaging in creative work allows you to externalize feelings that may be too difficult to verbalize, providing a safe outlet for stress, sadness, anger, and joy. This process can lead to significant emotional relief and insight, often bringing subconscious thoughts and feelings to the surface. Moreover, creating something truly yours can boost your self-esteem and provide a sense of accomplishment, reinforcing your identity and capabilities.

Exploring various forms of creative expression is vital to finding the medium that resonates deeply with you. "Whether it's through writing, where you can weave your emotions into words and narratives; painting, which allows you to splash your feelings in color across a canvas; music, where melodies and rhythms can echo your inner world; or dance, which lets your body express what words cannot;

each form of creativity offers a unique pathway to emotional expression. To discover what best suits you, allow yourself the freedom to experiment without judgment." Attend a pottery class, start a simple sketchbook, write poems or stories, or doodle in your spare time. Notice how each activity makes you feel, and look for the ones that bring you the most satisfaction and emotional release.

Integrating creativity into your daily life doesn't require monumental changes; it can be as simple as dedicating a small amount of time each day or week to your chosen creative activity. Create a small, inviting space in your home to engage with your art, be it a writing nook with a cozy chair and beautiful notebook or a corner of a room dedicated to painting or crafts. A physical space designated for creativity can motivate you to engage with your art regularly. Additionally, carry a small notebook or a sketchpad with you during the day. You never know when inspiration might strike or when a moment might arise where expressing yourself creatively can help manage stress or emotional upheaval.

Sharing your creative work can be both exhilarating and intimidating, but it also presents an opportunity to connect with others on a profound level. Sharing isn't about seeking approval or validation but expressing your truth and experiences. Finding that your work resonates with others can be incredibly validating, and this connection can foster a sense of community and support. However, sharing in environments where you feel safe and supported is essential. Start by sharing with close friends or family or in a community class where others expose their vulnerabilities through art. Online platforms can also be a powerful medium for sharing creativity, but be mindful of your emotional readiness to handle a broader audience. As you share your work, remember that the value lies not in the reception it receives but in the courage you showed in sharing your journey.

Through creative expression, you find a way to cope with your emotions and discover a path to understanding yourself better. This exploration can be enriching, adding richness and depth to your life. As you continue to engage with your creativity, you'll find it becomes more than just a method for emotional expression—it becomes a vital part of how you interact with the world, enhancing your perspective and enriching your experiences.

As this chapter concludes, reflect on how creativity serves as a bridge to express and manage your emotions and as a cornerstone in building a life filled with self-understanding and expressive richness. Each brushstroke, line written, or note played contributes to a broader canvas on which you are the artist of your life's story. Let these creative pursuits remind you of your resilience and beauty, and may they inspire you to continue exploring the depths of your imagination and emotions.

Please Share Your Experience and Make a Difference

YOUR WORDS CAN SPARK CHANGE!

"Happiness doesn't come from what you have but from what you give."

Unknown

When you share your thoughts and experiences, you help others find their way too. So, let's make a positive impact together!

Would you help someone just like you—curious about healing from toxic relationships but unsure where to start?

Our goal with **Lasting Toxic Relationship Recovery** is to make the journey to recovery clear and uplifting for everyone. But we need your help to reach more people.

Most people choose books based on reviews. So, we're asking you to support others on their path to healing by leaving a review.

It costs nothing and takes less than a minute but could significantly impact someone's recovery journey.

Your review could help***...one more person break free from harmful patterns. ...one more individual build healthier relationships. ...one more person rediscover their true self. ...one more life change for the better. ...one more dream of a fulfilling life come true.***

To make a difference, simply scan the QR code below and leave a review:

If you love helping others, you're the kind of person we appreciate most. Thank you from the bottom of our hearts!

Leslie and Kim Gowans

FIVE

Building Healthy Relationships

I magine stepping into a garden where each plant thrives, supported by rich soil and just the right amount of sunlight and water. This garden is a metaphor for a healthy relationship—a dynamic environment where mutual respect, trust, support, and honest communication are the nutrients that allow individuals to flourish. Transitioning from a toxic relationship to cultivating a healthy one can feel like learning a new language. Still, once you understand the fundamental elements that constitute a healthy relationship, you're equipped to nurture your interactions toward more fulfilling and sustaining connections.

The Anatomy of a Healthy Relationship: What Does it Look Like?

Healthy relationships are characterized by several key components, each serving a unique role in maintaining the relationship's overall health and vitality. Mutual respect is at the core of these relationships, which acts as the soil in our metaphorical garden. It involves honoring each other's feelings, desires, and needs and treating one another with consideration and kindness. When respect is mutual, both partners feel valued and acknowledged, creating a stable foundation for the relationship to grow.

Trust is another critical pillar of healthy relationships, akin to sunlight in our garden. It allows relationships to thrive by creating a sense of security and confidence between partners. Trust builds over time through consistent and reliable actions, honest communication, and the ability to be vulnerable with one another. It's the assurance that you can rely on your partner, that they will act with your best interests at heart, and that they will respect the boundaries and agreements within the relationship.

Support in a relationship is like the water that nourishes the garden —it's about being there for each other in times of growth and challenge. Supportive partners encourage each other's pursuits and are present through successes and failures without judgment. This attribute fosters an environment where both partners can express their true selves and pursue their personal goals, knowing they have a supportive base to return to.

Honest communication, the final essential element, acts as a vital and renewing air circulating through the garden. It involves sharing one's thoughts, feelings, and concerns openly and respectfully. Open communication helps prevent misunderstandings and resentments and allows partners to navigate conflicts and differences effectively. It requires active listening, empathy, and the willingness to understand perspectives different from one's own.

Real-Life Models of Healthy Relationships

To better understand these concepts, let's consider some real-life examples. Consider the relationship between former U.S. President Obama and his wife, Michelle. They demonstrate mutual respect by publicly acknowledging each other's achievements and strengths. Their trust is evident in their support for each other's career paths. Their effective communication is showcased during joint public appearances, where they interact with ease and genuine affection.

In literature, the relationship between Elizabeth Bennet and Mr. Darcy in Jane Austen's "Pride and Prejudice" evolves into mutual respect and trust. Throughout their journey, both characters learn to communicate their true feelings and listen to each other, overcoming initial misunderstandings and societal expectations to build a strong, supportive partnership.

Tools for Self-Evaluation

Understanding and nurturing these elements in your relationships starts with self-evaluation. One effective tool for this is the relationship health checklist. This checklist can include questions like: Do I feel respected by my partner? Do we trust each other? Are we supportive of each other's individual goals? How effectively do we communicate? Regularly reviewing this checklist can help you identify areas of strength and those needing improvement.

Another valuable tool is the trust scale, where you rate how much you trust your partner in various situations on a scale of one to ten. This can help pinpoint specific areas where trust could be strengthened.

By actively engaging with these tools and striving to foster respect, trust, support, and honest communication, you can cultivate a healthy relationship that survives and thrives. Like a well-tended garden, a healthy relationship can become a source of strength, beauty, and continual growth, enriching the lives of everyone it touches.

5.2 Communication Skills that Foster Understanding and Respect

Effective communication is the heartbeat of any thriving relationship, acting as the bridge that connects individuals by sharing thoughts, emotions, and experiences. Effective communication involves more than just talking; it encompasses active listening, the clear articulation of needs, and an awareness of non-verbal cues. Active listening requires you to fully concentrate, understand, respond, and remember what is being said. It's about being present in the conversation without planning your following response while the other person is speaking. This form of listening fosters more profound understanding and validates the speaker, making them feel heard and appreciated.

Articulating needs clearly is equally crucial. It involves expressing your thoughts and feelings openly and respectfully without leaving room for misinterpretation. This clarity prevents many misunderstandings that can escalate into conflicts. For instance, instead of saying, "You never listen to me," which is vague and accusatory, you could say, "I feel valued when you listen attentively to my concerns; lately, we have not had the opportunity to do that." This way, expressing your need for attention without blaming the other person is more likely to elicit a positive response.

Non-verbal communication, such as body language, eye contact, and facial expressions, also plays a pivotal role in receiving and interpreting messages. For example, crossed arms might be perceived as defensive or closed off, while maintaining eye contact can be seen as a sign of interest and honesty. Being mindful of your non-verbal cues and reading others' can significantly enhance communication, ensuring the message is heard and understood.

Avoiding Misunderstandings

Misunderstandings are often the root of many relationship problems, but they can be mitigated through specific communication strategies. Avoiding assumptions is critical; only assume you know what your partner means with clarification. Always ask questions if you need clarification on their words or actions. This practice helps prevent the buildup of misconceptions that can lead to resentment. Similarly, steering clear of generalizations such as "You always..." or "You never..." is essential because they distort reality, make the other person feel unfairly judged, and are likely to lead to defensive responses.

Passive-aggressive language, a common pitfall in many communications, can be particularly destructive. It involves expressing negative feelings indirectly rather than openly addressing an issue. Recognizing and eliminating such patterns from your communication can lead to more honest and productive interactions. Therefore, strive to express your feelings and needs directly and respectfully, fostering an atmosphere where issues can be discussed openly and resolved constructively.

Enhancing Empathy

Empathy—the ability to understand and share another person's feelings—is a cornerstone of effective communication and relationship building. It lets you see things from your partner's perspective and respond sensitively to their emotions. Cultivating empathy involves actively imagining how the other person feels in their situation, sometimes requiring setting aside your views and experiences to understand theirs better. This shift can dramatically improve how partners interact, transforming potential conflicts into bonding moments and deeper understanding.

Practicing empathy can be as simple as reflecting on what you've heard to show you understand. Phrases like "It sounds like you're feeling..." or "If I understand you correctly, you're saying..." help convey empathy. These reflective statements confirm that you are actively listening and allow the other person to clarify if you've misunderstood, promoting greater clarity and understanding.

Practical Exercises to Enhance Communication Skills

To put these concepts into practice, consider engaging in specific exercises with your partner or friends. One effective exercise is the 'Listening Swap.' Set a five-minute timer and allow one person to speak about something important to them while the other practices active listening. No interruptions are allowed; the listener should focus entirely on understanding the speaker's message. After the time is up, switch roles. This exercise can enhance your listening skills and demonstrate the value of giving undivided attention to someone else.

Another helpful activity is the 'Emotion Articulation Exercise.' Each person writes down a recent situation that evoked a strong emotional response. Take turns sharing your experiences, focusing on clearly articulating the emotions involved and the needs that arose from the situation. This exercise improves your ability to express your feelings clearly and helps develop empathy by sharing and understanding each other's emotional experiences.

By incorporating these skills and exercises into your daily interactions, you'll find that your ability to communicate effectively and empathetically will grow, paving the way for more meaningful and satisfying relationships. Whether with a partner, friend, or colleague, mastering the art of communication is a lifelong journey that can profoundly enrich your connections with others.

5.3 Recognizing and Reacting to Red Flags in New Relationships

In the early stages of a new relationship, it's easy to get swept up in the excitement and overlook subtle signs that might indicate underlying issues. However, paying attention to red flags early on can save you from potential heartache and more severe problems. Red flags are essentially warning signals—behaviors or traits exhibited by your partner that suggest underlying issues that could negatively impact the relationship. For instance, a quick temper can indicate poor emotional regulation, disrespect might reflect a fundamental lack of consideration for others, and over-control could signal more profound insecurity or mistrust. Recognizing these signs early allows you to address them before they become more significant problems.

Understanding and setting personal boundaries is crucial when navigating these red flags. Boundaries are the limits you set around behavior that you find acceptable or unacceptable in a relationship. They are essential for maintaining self-respect and ensuring the relationship thrives. When a red flag is raised, it's necessary to communicate your boundaries. Say your partner shows signs of a quick temper by snapping at you over minor issues; you might set a boundary by stating that while you understand everyone can have a bad day, speaking to you harshly is unacceptable. You expect conversations, even during disagreements, to be conducted respectfully. Setting this boundary early on informs your partner of your expectations and can help prevent a pattern of disrespect from developing.

When you notice red flags, addressing your concerns early in the relationship is beneficial. This proactive approach involves open and honest communication, expressing your feelings, and discussing your observations without accusation. For example, if your partner frequently makes plans without considering your schedule or preferences, bring this up directly. You might say, "I've noticed that my schedule wasn't considered the last few times we've made plans. I feel valued when we make decisions together. Can we discuss how we might better coordinate in the future?" This dialogue can help clarify whether these behaviors are mere oversight or part of a more troubling pattern of disregard for your needs and feelings.

If the red flags persist in some situations despite your best efforts, and the behavior doesn't change. In these cases, seeking external help from a counselor or mediator can be wise. These professionals can provide a neutral perspective and offer more effective strategies to deal with the issues. They can facilitate conversations that perhaps are too difficult for you to navigate alone, helping you and your partner better understand each other's perspectives and work towards a resolution. Engaging in couples therapy isn't an admission of defeat but rather a proactive, constructive step toward building a healthier relationship.

Addressing red flags isn't just about dealing with potential negatives; it's also about building a deeper understanding and stronger foundation for your relationship. Recognizing and reacting appropriately to these early warning signs sets the stage for open communication and mutual respect, which are critical to any healthy relationship. Whether it's through setting boundaries, having honest discussions, or seeking professional help, taking these steps shows a commitment to your well-being and the health of the relationship.

5.4 The Role of Emotional Intelligence in Relationship Success

Emotional Intelligence (EI), often measured as an Emotional Quotation (EQ), is the ability to understand, use, and manage your emotions positively to relieve stress, communicate effectively, empathize with others, overcome challenges, and defuse conflict. This ability is crucial in all spheres of life, especially in personal and romantic relationships, where emotional exchange is frequent and significant. EI involves a range of skills, including self-awareness, emotional regulation, and empathy, all vital in understanding your emotions and those around you.

Developing your emotional intelligence can fundamentally transform your approach to relationships. It starts with self-awareness, the ability to recognize your emotions and their impact on your thoughts and behavior. This awareness allows you to understand triggers that might affect your emotional state and to recognize the difference between feeling and acting. For example, you might feel jealous if your partner spends a lot of time with a friend, but remembering this emotion can help you decide how to express your feelings constructively rather than reacting impulsively.

Emotional regulation, another critical aspect of EI, refers to your ability to manage and redirect your emotions. This skill is essential in maintaining harmony in relationships. It involves techniques such as taking a deep breath when angry, calming yourself before responding to a situation, or even channeling negative energy into positive actions. Effective emotional regulation helps maintain a balanced perspective during emotional highs and lows, ensuring that your reactions contribute to healthy relationship dynamics rather than escalating conflicts.

Empathy is one of the most directly relational components of emotional intelligence. It is the ability to understand and share another person's feelings, which is foundational to developing compassion and a supportive relationship. Empathy allows you to see things from your partner's point of view and to respond to their needs without judgment. This understanding can deepen your connection and enhance mutual respect, reassuring your partner that their feelings and perspectives are valued and understood.

Emotional Intelligence in Action: Scenarios Demonstrating Emotional Intelligence

Consider a scenario where one partner comes home upset after a stressful day at work. An emotionally intelligent response involves recognizing the partner's distressed state, understanding that their mood might be more volatile, and responding with supportive behaviors rather than indifference or frustration. This might mean giving them space to unwind, listening to them vent without offering unsolicited advice, or doing something thoughtful to ease their stress. Such actions soothe the immediate situation and strengthen the relationship by reinforcing a bond of mutual support and understanding.

Another scenario might involve handling a disagreement about financial decisions. High EI contributes to a more productive discussion where both partners use clear, respectful communication and emotional regulation to express their perspectives. Instead of escalating into an argument, the situation becomes an opportunity to better understand each other's concerns and priorities, potentially leading to a compromise that respects both viewpoints. This resolves the immediate conflict and builds trust and resilience in the relationship by demonstrating that differences can be handled constructively.

Benefits of Emotional Intelligence

The benefits of cultivating emotional intelligence are profound and far-reaching. Enhanced EI improves communication by helping you convey your thoughts and emotions clearly and listen more effectively. It also enhances conflict resolution skills by providing you with tools to approach disagreements with empathy and a calm, clear head. Moreover, high EI can deepen emotional connections between partners by fostering an environment of mutual understanding and respect. It encourages a nurturing, supportive, and empathetic relationship dynamic, which is conducive to long-term relationship satisfaction and stability.

By investing time in developing your emotional intelligence, you not only improve your emotional health but also contribute to a healthier, more fulfilling relationship. The skills gained through enhancing your EI—self-awareness, emotional regulation, and empathy—are essential tools for navigating the complexities of intimate relationships. They enable you to build stronger bonds, handle challenges more effectively, and create a supportive and loving environment for you and your partner. As you continue to grow your emotional intelligence, you'll find that its benefits permeate all areas of your life, enhancing not just romantic relationships but also friendships, family dynamics, and professional interactions.

5.5 Maintaining Individuality and Independence in Partnerships

In the dance of partnership, it's all too easy for lines to blur, for individual colors to wash into a shared hue that obscures where one ends and the other begins. Yet, maintaining your distinctiveness—not just your hobbies but your dreams and your growth—is not a luxury; it's essential. It's the very essence that keeps the relationship vibrant and healthy. When individuals nourish their identities, they bring richness and variety into their relationships, enhancing their shared experiences by contributing unique perspectives and strengths. This dynamic allows both partners to feel fulfilled within themselves and their relationship, reducing dependency and the potential resentment that often follows when one feels lost or subsumed by the partnership.

Balancing the "we" and the "me" might sound straightforward, but it requires conscious effort and ongoing negotiation within the relationship. It starts with communicating, expressing your needs, and listening to your partner. From there, it's about giving each other space to pursue personal ambitions and interests. For instance, if one partner enjoys photography and the other likes hiking, supporting each other's interests could mean arranging a time to attend a photography class while the other explores new trails. This not only shows mutual respect and interests but also allows both partners to miss each other and experience life independently, which can rejuvenate both the individual spirit and the relationship.

Encouraging one another to indulge in personal hobbies and interests plays a crucial role in maintaining this balance. It's about celebrating each other's passions and successes as individual achievements. When partners champion each other's growth, the relationship becomes a source of inspiration, a base from which individuals can confidently explore the world. This support can be as simple as asking about a partner's day and listening genuinely, attending exhibitions or performances showcasing a partner's talents, or allocating a budget for personal development courses. Each gesture, no matter how small, reinforces the value of the individual within the partnership.

Case Studies of Successful Independent Partnerships

Consider the story of Maya and Alex, both passionate about their careers, Maya in law and Alex in academia. Early in their relationship, they agreed on a simple yet powerful ritual: "Career Fridays," where they would share updates about their work, discuss challenges, and celebrate achievements. This ritual became a cornerstone of their relationship, a weekly reminder of their support for each other's professional journeys.

Then there's Priya and Sam, who shared a love for travel but often had different destinations in mind. Instead of compromising on every trip, they occasionally traveled solo or with friends who shared their specific interests. This arrangement allowed them both to pursue their travel passions without restraint, enriching their individual experiences and the stories they could share.

These examples underscore that maintaining individuality doesn't detract from the partnership; rather, it enriches and deepens the connection by fostering an environment of mutual respect and support. Partners who embrace their individuality while nurturing their relationship create a dynamic, resilient bond and are better equipped to grow and adapt over time. This balance isn't achieved overnight but through continuous, conscious efforts that affirm the value of both the individual and the couple, ensuring that both thrive.

5.6 Conflict Resolution Strategies that Promote Growth

Recognizing that conflict is a natural and inevitable relationship component is fundamental. Far from being a sign that something is inherently wrong, conflicts can indicate that each person actively engages and invests in the relationship, bringing their perspectives and desires to the fore. It is not the presence of conflict that destabilizes relationships but how it is handled. Addressed constructively, conflict can become a powerful catalyst for growth, fostering more profound understanding and strengthening bonds between partners.

One of the most effective techniques for healthy conflict resolution is the use of 'I' statements. This approach focuses on expressing your experiences and feelings rather than attributing blame or intent to the other person. For instance, saying, "I feel overlooked when decisions are made without my input," instead of "You never consider my opinions," can make a significant difference. This method not only reduces defensiveness but also promotes open, honest communication. By framing your concerns around your reactions and needs, you invite your partner into your emotional world, sharing how specific actions affect you without casting aspersions on their character or intentions.

Taking timeouts is another vital strategy, mainly when emotions run high. During intense conflicts, it's easy for stress levels to escalate, leading to reactions that can exacerbate the situation. By agreeing to take a brief break, you allow yourself time to cool down, reflect, and gather your thoughts. This pause can be the difference between a resolution and a regrettable escalation. It's important during these timeouts to focus on calming yourself and reflecting on the issue at hand rather than ruminating on your anger or rehearsing your following argument. When both partners return to the discussion, they are often more composed and ready to engage constructively.

Another crucial element is focusing on solutions rather than problems. Shift the conversation from what went wrong to how you can prevent similar issues in the future. This shift doesn't mean ignoring the problem but viewing it as a mutual challenge to overcome together. Start by clearly defining the problem, then brainstorm possible solutions, weigh their pros and cons, and decide on a course of action that both feel is fair. This collaborative approach solves the immediate issue and strengthens your teamwork and problem-solving skills as a couple.

Learning from Disagreements

Every conflict offers a unique window into the inner workings of your partner's mind, presenting opportunities to understand their values, fears, and pressures. Viewing disagreements as learning opportunities can transform how you perceive conflicts, seeing them not as threats but as chances to enrich your relationship. For example, a dispute over spending habits can reveal deeper priorities about security and lifestyle choices, which, once understood, can lead to more empathetic interactions and aligned goals.

The key is to maintain curiosity about your partner's perspective throughout conflicts. Ask questions to clarify their points and listen actively. This openness alleviates the conflict and deepens your mutual understanding, instrumental in building a resilient, enduring relationship.

Preventing Escalation

Preventing conflicts from escalating into damaging fights is crucial. Start by recognizing early warning signs in yourself and your partner. These might include raised voices, quickened breathing, or an agitated demeanor. When you notice these signs, it's a cue to slow down and employ de-escalation techniques like those mentioned— taking timeouts, using 'I' statements, or shifting the focus to solutions.

It is also vital to address issues preemptively before they fester. Regular check-ins can be helpful, where you can share grievances in a non-confrontational setting, ensuring minor problems are discussed before they become more significant. This proactive communication helps keep the relationship's emotional climate in check, making it easier to deal with conflicts as they arise.

By embracing these strategies, conflicts can transform from dreaded encounters to opportunities for growth and deepening intimacy. They allow you to explore the complexities of your relationship and the personal growth that comes from navigating these challenges together. This perspective doesn't just resolve conflicts; it enriches your relationship, making it more dynamic and resilient in the face of future challenges.

As we conclude this chapter, remember that the strategies discussed here are theoretical ideals and practical tools that can help forge stronger bonds. From understanding the natural role of conflict in relationships to employing specific techniques for healthy resolutions, these insights equip you with the skills necessary for nurturing a supportive, understanding, and loving relationship. As we transition into the next chapter, we will build on these foundations, exploring advanced strategies for ensuring long-term relationship success and satisfaction.

SIX

Advanced Strategies for Long-Term Success

I magine you're climbing a mountain. You've pushed through the initial rough terrain and the exhilarating thrill of starting a new ascent, and now, you're facing the long, demanding stretch that leads to the summit. This part of the climb requires physical endurance and a strategic approach to manage resources, maintain your pace, and keep your motivation burning despite the fatigue that inevitably creeps in. Similarly, in the journey of personal development and self-improvement after leaving a toxic relationship, the initial relief and empowerment can gradually give way to the challenges of sustaining growth and avoiding burnout. This chapter equips you with advanced strategies to ensure that your journey toward healing and self-discovery isn't a fleeting endeavor, but rather a sustainable, life-long process.

6.1 Sustainable Self-Improvement: Avoiding Burnout

Burnout can subtly infiltrate your life, particularly when you're deeply committed to personal growth and improvement. It manifests in signs that are easy to overlook: exhaustion that a good night's sleep doesn't cure, a creeping sense of disillusionment about goals that once sparked a passion or a persistent feeling of stagnation. Recognizing these early signs is crucial. Exhaustion might be physical, emotional, or mental, reflecting the deep energy reserves you've been tapping into. Disillusionment can make you question the value of your efforts, casting a shadow over your achievements. Stagnation, or the feeling that you're running in place, often suggests that your strategies need recalibration to match your evolving needs and circumstances.

Balancing ambition with wellness is fundamental to preventing burnout. Ambition drives you to set goals and strive towards them, but without the counterbalance of wellness, it's akin to running a marathon at a sprinter's pace. To maintain this balance, set realistic, achievable goals that challenge you without pushing you to the brink. Integrate regular breaks and self-care routines into your schedule. These aren't just pauses; think of them as times for recovery and reflection, which are essential for sustained effort. Engage in activities that replenish your energy and bring you joy, whether it's a hobby, spending time with loved ones, or simply resting. Remember, productivity isn't just about doing more; it's about maintaining the ability to perform well over the long term.

Continuous Learning and Adaptation

In the realm of personal development, the only constant is change. The strategies that worked for you at the beginning of your journey might not be as effective as you evolve and grow. Embrace continuous learning as a way to adapt to these changes. This might mean updating your knowledge base, learning new skills, or even changing your direction as you gain deeper insights into yourself and your goals. Adaptation also involves letting go of what no longer serves you, which can be as significant as adopting new approaches.

Interactive Element: Journaling Prompt

Reflect on a goal or strategy you've been pursuing for a while. Is it still serving you, or does it feel like you're holding onto it out of habit or obligation? Write about this goal and whether it aligns with your values and aspirations.

Community support plays an indispensable role in sustainable self-improvement. It can transform the often lonely road of personal growth into a shared journey, enriching your experience and providing a network of motivation and support. Engage with communities, whether they are online forums, local clubs, or support groups that align with your interests and goals. These communities offer emotional support, practical advice, and resources to help you navigate your path more effectively. They remind you that you are not alone in your struggles and that others share your aspirations and challenges. This sense of belonging can be a powerful antidote to the isolation that sometimes accompanies intensive personal growth efforts.

As you equip yourself with these strategies, remember that the goal of self-improvement isn't to strive without reprieve perpetually but to build a fulfilling life that reflects your deepest values and aspirations. By recognizing the signs of burnout, balancing ambition with wellness, continuously learning and adapting, and leveraging community support, you ensure your journey is successful, sustainable, and enriching. Carry these strategies with you as you climb towards your summit, knowing that each step is part of a more excellent journey that shapes what you achieve and who you become.

6.2 Navigating Dating Apps and Social Media Wisely

In the digital age, the quest for companionship often leads us to the virtual doorsteps of dating apps and social media platforms. While these tools have revolutionized dating, offering convenience and vast choices, they require you to navigate new challenges and dynamics. Setting healthy, realistic expectations is your first strategy in making these digital tools work for you, not against you. It's easy to get swept up by beautifully curated profiles and the illusion of endless options, but remember, genuine connections are built on more than just digital chemistry. Expecting instant sparks or believing that every interaction should lead to a meaningful relationship can set you up for disappointment and frustration. Instead, approach these platforms with curiosity and openness without the heavy burden of immediate outcomes.

This mindset also helps manage discrepancies between online personas and real-life personalities. People commonly present an idealized version of themselves online, leading to mismatched expectations when you meet in person. Setting realistic expectations prepares you mentally and emotionally for this possibility, reducing potential disappointment. Use these platforms to learn more about your preferences, communication styles, and what you seek in a partner. Each interaction, whether it leads to a romantic connection or not, is valuable in honing your understanding of the type of relationship that best suits you.

Maintaining privacy and safety on dating apps and social media is also paramount. In the excitement of connecting with new people, it's crucial not to overshare information too soon. Personal details such as your home address, place of work, financial information, or any other sensitive data should be guarded until a significant level of trust is established. Start by sharing general details about your life and interests, and observe how the other person handles this information. Are they respectful of your boundaries? Do they reciprocate by sharing at a similar pace, or do they press for more detailed information prematurely? These interactions can indicate their respect for your privacy and boundaries.

Privacy and Safety Tips

- Always meet in public places for the first few times.
- Inform a friend or family member about your plans when meeting someone from an app.
- Use the communication tools on the dating app rather than immediately giving out your phone number.
- Listen to your instincts—do not hesitate to cut off communication if something feels off.

Recognizing red flags in online interactions is another critical skill. Be wary of profiles or messages that seem too good to be true—they often are. Inconsistencies in stories, vague or evasive answers to specific questions, or any behavior that seems overly controlling or demanding should raise immediate concerns. For instance, someone who pushes to move conversations off the dating platform to more private channels like texting or email right away might not have honest intentions. Another red flag is rushed intimacy; someone declaring strong feelings or pushing for a serious relationship without adequate time or mutual interaction does not respect the natural pacing of relationship development. These behaviors indicate manipulative tactics or scams, unfortunately too familiar in online dating environments.

Balancing online and offline interactions is the final key to building genuine connections. While online platforms are effective for initial introductions and getting to know basic information about someone, face-to-face interactions provide deeper insights into their personality and your mutual chemistry. Encourage moving from chatting online to meeting in safe, public spaces when both parties feel comfortable. This transition can reveal much about the person's social skills, manners, and how they treat others, which are critical components of a potential relationship. Additionally, real-world dates allow you to observe non-verbal cues and behaviors that are impossible to gauge through screens, providing a fuller picture of the person's character and compatibility with you.

In navigating the complex world of dating apps and social media, remember that these tools are just that—tools. They are not a replacement for the organic development of relationships but rather a means to facilitate introductions and connections. By setting realistic expectations, prioritizing safety and privacy, recognizing red flags, and balancing online interactions with real-world meetings, you equip yourself to manage these platforms wisely, increasing your chances of forming meaningful and lasting relationships.

6.3 The Importance of Reciprocity in Love and Relationships

In the intricate dance of relationships, reciprocity is the rhythm that keeps the movements synchronized and harmonious. At its core, reciprocity in relationships refers to the mutual exchange of emotions, efforts, and support, ensuring that both partners contribute and receive equally. This balance is crucial for maintaining a healthy relationship and fostering an environment where both individuals can thrive and grow. When both partners feel their needs are being met and their contributions valued, it enhances their satisfaction and deepens their connection.

However, achieving this balance is only sometimes straightforward. Recognizing signs of imbalance is the first step toward fostering healthier interactions. Imbalance can manifest in various ways, such as one partner consistently making more effort to maintain the relationship, whether in terms of emotional support, financial contributions, or even the mundane tasks of daily living. This disproportion often leads to resentment and dissatisfaction, which, if left unchecked, can erode the foundation of the relationship. You might notice signs like feeling drained after interactions with your partner, or you might frequently compromise your needs or desires to accommodate theirs without reciprocation. These feelings are indicators that the reciprocity in your relationship may be off-kilter.

To foster reciprocal interactions, open communication about needs and expectations is essential. This involves having honest discussions about what each partner needs from the relationship and how both can work towards fulfilling these needs. For example, discussing how the other can provide that support can make a significant difference if one partner needs more emotional support. It's also important to actively work on meeting each other's needs. This doesn't mean keeping a score but showing willingness to be there for each other and share responsibilities fairly. Regular check-ins can be beneficial here, providing a space to discuss how each partner feels about the balance of give and take in the relationship and to adjust as needed.

Dealing with a partner who is consistently non-reciprocal requires a careful approach. Initially, attempt to address the issue with open communication, expressing how the imbalance affects you and the relationship. Sometimes, partners may not be aware of the disparity, and this conversation can prompt a positive change. However, if discussions don't lead to improvement, it might be necessary to reassess the relationship. A continuous lack of reciprocity can lead to a one-sided, unhealthy, or unsustainable relationship. In such cases, consider seeking advice from a counselor who can provide guidance tailored to your situation. They can offer strategies to attempt to balance the relationship or help you come to terms with the possibility that the healthiest option might be to part ways.

Navigating the complexities of relationship reciprocity is fundamental to building and maintaining lasting, satisfying partnerships. Recognizing signs of imbalance, communicating openly about individual needs, and being willing to adjust behaviors can ensure you and your partner feel valued and supported. Remember, a relationship thrives on mutual give and take; fostering this balance is key to creating a loving, supportive, and fulfilling connection with your partner.

6.4 Boundary Setting with Family and Friends

In the intricate web of our daily lives, the boundaries we set with family and friends are like the personal guidelines that dictate the quality of our interactions. These boundaries are not just lines in the sand meant to keep others out; they are expressions of our needs and values, crucial for our well-being and the health of our relationships. Setting boundaries helps define how we want to be treated by others, what we are comfortable with, and where we draw the line on unacceptable behaviors. This clarity is essential for maintaining personal integrity and mutually respectful and supportive relationships.

Establishing boundaries with family and friends begins with self-reflection. Identify the areas where you feel discomfort, resentment, or frustration in your relationships. These emotions are often indicators that a boundary needs to be set. For example, if you feel drained after visits from a particular family member who usually brings up negative topics, setting a boundary around the topics of conversation when they visit can help preserve your emotional energy. Communicating these boundaries clearly and respectfully is critical. Approach the discussion with a focus on your needs rather than their faults. Use "I" statements to express how certain behaviors affect you and specify what you need instead. For instance, you might say, "I feel overwhelmed when we discuss these topics. I'd appreciate it if we could focus on more positive subjects during our visits."

Handling resistance is an inevitable part of setting boundaries. Not everyone will initially understand or respect your limits, and some may react negatively. It's important to stay firm and calm in these situations. Reiterate your boundaries and explain why they are essential to you. If someone continuously disrespects your boundaries, you may need to enforce consequences, such as reducing the frequency of contact with them. This isn't about punishment; it's about protecting your well-being. It's also helpful to provide context, helping them understand that these boundaries are not just whims but essential elements of your relationship with them. For example, explaining that you value your time with them more when conversations are positive can help them see the benefit of respecting your boundaries.

Maintaining boundaries over the long term requires consistency. Regularly review your boundaries and assess whether they still serve your needs or need adjustments—life changes and our needs and relationships. An open dialogue about boundaries should be maintained in regular interactions with family and friends. This ongoing communication helps prevent misunderstandings and ensures everyone is clear about expectations. It's also crucial to model the respect for boundaries you expect from others. You set a standard for mutual respect and understanding in all your relationships by respecting their limits.

Setting and maintaining healthy boundaries with those close to you might feel challenging, especially if you're not used to asserting your needs. However, the clarity that comes from having well-defined boundaries is liberating. It allows you to interact with loved ones in a way that preserves and enhances your well-being and strengthens your relationships. As you continue to navigate the complex dynamics of family and friendship, remember that setting boundaries is not a barrier but a bridge to healthier, more fulfilling interactions.

6.5 Long-Term Goal Setting for Personal and Relationship Growth

Setting long-term goals is akin to planting seeds for your future; it requires vision, care, and patience. Whether these goals pertain to personal achievements or the growth of your relationships, they serve as vital benchmarks that guide your actions and decisions. The benefits of setting these goals extend beyond merely reaching them—they imbue your daily life with purpose, direction, and motivation. Imagine each goal as a lighthouse, providing light on your path and guiding you through foggy uncertainties. This clarity of direction is essential, especially after navigating the stormy waters of toxic relationships. It helps rebuild a sense of identity and personal agency, which are crucial for recovery and growth.

Long-term goals also offer a profound sense of accomplishment once they are achieved. This isn't just about checking a box on your to-do list; it's about celebrating the journey and the personal growth that occurred along the way. Each achieved goal is a testament to your resilience and commitment to improving your life and relationships. These successes, big or small, boost your self-esteem and reinforce your belief in your ability to influence your own life positively.

Incorporating effective goal-setting frameworks can significantly enhance the process of establishing and reaching your long-term goals. One of the most recognized and effective methodologies is the SMART criteria, where goals are designed to be Specific, Measurable, Achievable, Relevant, and Time-bound. Applying this framework to your goals can transform them from vague wishes, to clear actionable objectives. For instance, instead of setting a goal to "be happier," a SMART goal would be "to dedicate at least two hours per week to mindfulness and meditation practices to improve my mental health by the end of the next three months." This goal is specific (mindfulness and meditation), measurable (two hours per week), achievable (a reasonable amount of time per week), relevant (improves mental health), and time-bound (by the end of three months).

Regular Review and Adjustment of Goals

Life is dynamic, and your circumstances and understanding of your needs and wants can change. That's why reviewing your goals regularly—perhaps quarterly or biannually—is crucial to ensure they align with your current situation and aspirations. This regular reassessment allows you to adjust your course, refine your strategies, or set new goals that better match your evolved outlook. For example, if a relationship goal was initially to improve communication with your partner through weekly discussions, but you find these discussions are needed more frequently, adjust the goal to reflect this new insight. This flexibility in managing your goals not only keeps them relevant but also keeps you engaged and responsive to your own developmental needs.

Integrating long-term goals into daily life is essential for maintaining momentum and ensuring consistent progress. Break down your larger goals into smaller, manageable tasks that can be incorporated into your everyday routine. For example, set a daily word count target if you want to write a book. To build a healthier relationship, designate regular times for open dialogue or shared activities with your partner. These small steps accumulate, creating gradual but steady progress and significantly reducing the overwhelming feeling of pursuing larger aspirations.

Additionally, integrate reminders of your goals into your environment. Use tools like planners, apps, or visual representations like vision boards in your workspace or home. These serve as continual prompts and motivators, keeping you focused and proactive.

Setting thoughtful, well-structured long-term goals gives direction and purpose to your personal and relational growth. It enhances your capacity to achieve and exceed what you might have thought possible. You actively shape your future through these goals, crafting a life that reflects your deepest values and aspirations. Each step in this direction is toward a more fulfilling and empowered existence.

6.6 Celebrating Milestones and Successes in Recovery

Recognizing and celebrating milestones in your recovery and personal growth is like marking the waypoints on a map during a long hike. These markers are not just about how far you've come; they remind you that every step is integral to a broader transformation. It is crucial to identify these milestones—whether they're small successes like maintaining no contact with a toxic ex for a month or significant achievements like establishing a new healthy relationship. They are tangible evidence of your progress and contribute to building a positive self-image.

To effectively recognize these milestones, start by setting clear criteria for a milestone in your journey. This could be anything from emotional breakthroughs, such as successfully managing a trigger, to practical achievements, such as completing a course that enhances personal or professional growth. The key is acknowledging the big and small successes and understanding that each plays a significant role in your recovery. Regular reflection can aid in this process. For example, at the end of each month, take a moment to jot down all the positive steps you've taken. This helps recognize your progress and sets goals for the coming months.

Celebration techniques can vary widely, but the essence lies in choosing activities that reinforce these positive changes and make you feel valued. For some, this means a quiet evening reflecting on the journey and journaling about the experiences and lessons learned. For others, it could involve a public acknowledgment, like a small gathering with close friends or family who have supported you. How you celebrate should resonate with your tastes and current needs, making the experience genuinely rewarding.

Sharing your successes with others can be profoundly impactful, not just for you but also for those around you. It strengthens social bonds and provides external validation of your efforts. When you share your achievements, be selective about the audience—choose people who have shown genuine support and interest in your well-being. This might be a trusted friend, a family member, or a support group. Sharing allows you to express gratitude for their support and inspires others on a similar path. It transforms individual success into a shared source of inspiration, reinforcing the communal bonds essential in times of personal change.

Reflective Practices Post-Celebration

After the celebration winds down, engaging in reflective practices can provide deep insights into your growth journey. Reflect on what these achievements mean and how they align with your goals. Consider your challenges, how you overcame them, and what you might do differently. This reflection can be facilitated through writing, meditation, or even discussions with a mentor or therapist.

The act of reflection not only deepens your understanding of your growth patterns but also prepares you for future challenges. By assessing the strategies that worked and those that didn't, you refine your approach to continuing personal development. This ongoing cycle of action, celebration, and reflection creates a powerful momentum that can propel you towards even more significant achievements, ensuring that your recovery and growth are not momentary and sustained over the long term.

As this chapter closes, remember that each step forward, each milestone reached, and each success celebrated, big or small, is a testament to your strength and resilience. These moments are not just marks of progress but beacons of hope that light your path forward. They remind you that change is possible, recovery is within reach, and your efforts are worthwhile. As you continue to navigate the complexities of healing and growth, let these celebrations be your guideposts, affirming that each step you take is toward a brighter, more fulfilling future.

The next chapter will explore dealing with setbacks and challenges that inevitably arise in any significant change journey. This next phase equips you with the resilience and strategies to face these challenges and emerge stronger.

SEVEN

Special Topics in Toxic Relationship Recovery

I magine stepping into your workplace, where you're expected to thrive and contribute your best, only to find yourself constantly dodging negativity, manipulation, or outright hostility. It's a scenario with far too many faces, turning what should be a productive and fulfilling environment into a battlefield of emotional and mental endurance. This chapter delves into the complex world of toxic relationships within professional settings, offering you strategies and insights to cope and reclaim your professional integrity and well-being.

7.1 Dealing with Toxic Relationships at Work

Navigating the choppy waters of toxic relationships at work requires a keen eye for recognizing harmful behaviors that go beyond the occasional bad day or regular stress-induced outburst. Toxicity in the workplace can manifest in various forms, ranging from subtle manipulations to overt bullying and abuse of power. These behaviors disrupt workplace harmony and can significantly hinder professional and personal growth.

Manipulation at work often appears under the guise of camaraderie or authority. A manipulative colleague or boss might use their influence to sway your decisions, undermine your job, or coerce you into taking on unreasonable workloads without proper acknowledgment. Overt and covert bullying in professional settings can be identified through consistent patterns of humiliation, intentional exclusion, and the spreading of malicious rumors. Abuse of power is particularly detrimental, involving actions where superiors exploit their position to intimidate or control others, often pressuring employees to act against their ethical standards or personal comfort.

Establishing and maintaining professional boundaries is crucial to managing these toxic dynamics effectively. Clear boundaries help define acceptable behaviors and interactions, ensuring a respectful work environment. Communicate your boundaries assertively, ensuring you are clear about what you will not tolerate and the consequences of those actions. Documenting incidents is another critical strategy. Detailed records of toxic interactions provide a factual basis for addressing the issues, whether in mediation sessions or formal complaints and protect you against possible retaliation.

Utilizing HR processes is vital when dealing with workplace toxicity. Human Resources departments are equipped to handle such issues and can provide guidance and intervention. Reporting toxic behavior helps address the problem and contributes to a healthier workplace culture, discouraging such dynamics and promoting a safe environment for everyone.

Maintaining professional integrity in the face of toxic relationships is challenging yet essential. It involves adhering to your ethical standards and not allowing the toxic behavior of others to influence your professional conduct. Preserve your mental well-being by engaging in regular self-care practices, such as mindfulness exercises, professional development, and seeking emotional support outside work. This helps in building resilience against the negative impacts of toxicity.

Seeking external support plays a crucial role in managing workplace toxicity. Mentors and industry networks provide professional guidance and emotional support, helping you navigate challenging situations. They can offer valuable perspectives and advice based on their experiences, which is instrumental in developing effective coping strategies for toxic relationships at work. Additionally, professional counselors can assist in addressing the emotional and psychological stress caused by toxic work environments, providing tools to manage stress and maintain your well-being.

Interactive Element: Reflective Journaling Prompt

Consider the following questions to explore your experiences and feelings about toxicity in the workplace:

- How have toxic relationships at work affected your professional and personal life?
- What boundaries might you set to protect your well-being and integrity at work?
- Reflect on a situation where you dealt with a toxic colleague or superior. What strategies did you use, and what would you do differently now?

This reflective exercise encourages you to think critically about your workplace dynamics and to consider practical steps toward creating a healthier work environment. By recognizing toxic behaviors and implementing effective strategies, you empower yourself to foster a professional setting that supports your growth, well-being, and success.

7.2 Parenting and Co-Parenting Amidst Toxic Ex-Partners

Navigating the complexities of parenting alongside a toxic ex-partner demands a delicate balance of firm boundaries and flexible strategies, always with the well-being of the children at heart. When co-parenting in such circumstances, the challenges can seem monumental, but with suitable approaches, you can minimize conflict and create a stable environment for your children. The key is to focus on managing interactions with your ex and fostering a nurturing space for your children to thrive.

Establishing a structured framework for interaction can significantly reduce the potential for conflict. This involves setting clear, agreed-upon guidelines for communication. Opt for written forms of communication, such as emails or texts, which can prevent immediate emotional reactions and provide a record of exchanges. Utilize neutral communication tools for co-parenting, like shared online calendars for scheduling children's activities or apps that organize medical information, school events, and other vital data. This helps keep parents informed without direct contact and minimizes misunderstandings and miscommunications.

Legal and practical considerations are crucial in navigating co-parenting with a toxic ex-partner. Legal counsel can provide guidance tailored to your situation, helping you understand your parental rights and responsibilities. Legal interventions such as adjusted custody arrangements or supervised visitations may be necessary when interactions harm your or your children's well-being. Furthermore, involving a neutral third party for mediation can be beneficial. Mediators resolve disputes by facilitating a constructive dialogue between co-parents to reach mutually agreeable solutions, focusing on the children's best interests.

Supporting children amid co-parenting challenges is paramount. Children are often sensitive to parental tensions and may feel torn between their loyalties to both parents. It's essential to communicate with your children in age-appropriate ways, reassuring them that both parents love them and that the separation is not their fault. Encourage your children to express their feelings and provide them with the support they need to process those emotions, such as counseling or therapy if necessary. Activities that promote emotional expression, like art or writing, can also be therapeutic for children. Moreover, maintaining consistency in routines and discipline between households provides children stability and security, helping them adapt to the changes more resiliently.

Self-care emerges as a critical strategy for your well-being and as a model for your children. Managing co-parenting stress effectively requires taking care of your physical and emotional health. Engage in regular physical activity, which can improve your mood and reduce stress, and connect with supportive friends, family, or support groups who understand your challenges and provide emotional comfort and practical advice. Prioritizing your well-being helps you maintain the energy, patience, and clarity needed to handle the demands of co-parenting with a toxic ex-partner.

By employing these strategies, you can navigate the intricacies of co-parenting in a way that protects your children's well-being and supports your own mental and emotional health. Through structured communication, legal safeguards, focused support for your children, and diligent self-care, you create a framework within which your children can grow and flourish despite the complexities of dealing with a toxic ex-partner.

7.3 The Intersection of Culture and Toxic Relationships

Culture profoundly influences how individuals perceive, experience, and manage relationships. The fabric of one's cultural background weaves its patterns not just in celebrations and rituals but deeply into the personal realms of relationships, including toxic ones. Across various cultures, the dynamics of toxic relationships can be perceived and handled distinctively, influenced by cultural norms, values, and expectations.

In some cultures, the stigma associated with leaving a relationship, no matter how harmful, may deter individuals from seeking help or exiting unhealthy situations. This stigma is often intertwined with traditional beliefs about family honor, marital permanence, and social reputation, making it challenging for those involved to pursue separation or divorce without fear of societal backlash or familial disapproval.

Family expectations also play a pivotal role in how toxic relationships are managed within different cultural contexts. In collectivist societies, where family cohesion and honor are highly valued, individuals might be pressured to maintain appearances or suppress personal grievances for family unity. This cultural pressure can lead to prolonged suffering in silence, with the individual's well-being often overshadowed by the perceived need to uphold family honor. In more individualistic societies, there may be a greater emphasis on personal happiness and autonomy, providing a supportive backdrop for individuals to leave toxic relationships and seek personal fulfillment.

The variations in handling toxic relationships across cultures are not merely academic observations but realities that significantly impact individuals' lives. For instance, in some Eastern cultures, the 'saving face' concept might prevent individuals from discussing personal issues like relationship problems outside the family circle, limiting their access to support and resources. On the other hand, Western cultures might offer more open discussions about such issues. However, they could still perpetuate certain stigmas, such as the notion that one should have recognized the signs of toxicity earlier, which can lead to feelings of shame or guilt.

Navigating the path to healing from toxic relationships requires an understanding of cultural competence and acknowledging how cultural identity shapes the recovery process. Culturally sensitive approaches to healing recognize and respect an individual's cultural background and its influence on their relationship dynamics. These approaches encourage the integration of cultural beliefs and values into the healing process, making it more relevant and effective. For instance, therapy sessions that respect and incorporate an individual's cultural expressions of distress or healing can foster a deeper understanding and a more supportive therapeutic environment.

Understanding the intersection of culture and toxic relationships is crucial for creating effective support systems and therapeutic practices. By acknowledging and addressing the cultural dimensions that influence these relationships, we can better support individuals in their journey toward healing and empowerment.

Resources and Support for Diverse Populations

Identifying and highlighting resources and support networks tailored to diverse cultural backgrounds is crucial in providing practical help to those navigating the aftermath of toxic relationships. Community centers, cultural associations, and religious groups can serve as valuable support networks, offering a sense of belonging and a safe space to discuss and address relationship issues within a culturally understanding framework. These organizations often provide access to resources such as counseling, legal advice, and support groups that are culturally attuned, enhancing their accessibility and relevance.

Online platforms and resources that focus on multicultural education and support can also play a significant role in aiding recovery. Websites and forums that discuss relationship dynamics within specific cultural contexts can offer insights and support that resonate more deeply with individuals from those backgrounds. Additionally, books and publications that address the intersection of culture and relationship issues can provide valuable perspectives and coping strategies that consider cultural nuances.

Fostering a network of culturally competent professionals who understand diverse populations' specific needs and challenges is also essential. This network can include therapists, counselors, and social workers trained in culturally sensitive practices who can navigate the complexities of culture-related issues in toxic relationships and offer appropriate support and interventions.

By understanding and integrating the cultural dimensions of toxic relationships, individuals and communities can better support those affected, promoting healing practices that are both effective and respectful of cultural identities. This holistic approach acknowledges and embraces cultural diversity, leading to more compassionate and inclusive support systems that empower individuals to recover and thrive after toxic relationships.

7.4 Healing from a Toxic Relationship Without Professional Help

In the aftermath of a toxic relationship, the path to healing can sometimes feel like navigating a dense, unfamiliar forest without a map. However, not everyone has the resources or the desire to seek professional help, and that's perfectly okay. You can still find your way to recovery through self-help strategies that empower you to regain control of your emotional well-being. Self-education, for instance, is a powerful tool. By learning about the dynamics of toxic relationships and understanding the psychological impacts they can have, you equip yourself with knowledge that can demystify your experiences and validate your feelings. Resources like books, reputable online articles, and educational videos can provide a solid foundation of knowledge, helping you recognize patterns you might have missed and understand that you're not alone in what you've experienced.

Peer support groups are another invaluable resource. These groups bring together individuals who have faced similar challenges, providing a collective of experiences and wisdom to draw from. Participating in these groups can give you a sense of community and belonging, which is incredibly healing. Sharing stories and successes can inspire and motivate you, while the communal empathy can soothe your emotional wounds. Whether online or in person, these groups create a safe space to express your feelings and receive support without judgment, making the healing journey less isolating.

Guided self-reflection is a powerful personal practice that involves looking inward to understand your thoughts, emotions, and behaviors. This can be facilitated through mindfulness techniques, meditation, or journaling. By regularly setting aside time to reflect, you allow yourself to process the complex emotions that arise from toxic relationships. Journaling, in particular, offers a private, uncensored medium to pour out your thoughts and feelings, which can be incredibly cathartic. It also serves as a tangible record of your healing journey, allowing you to see how far you've come over time, which can be incredibly affirming.

Building a personal support network is crucial when healing on your own. This network should include friends and family members who are supportive and understanding of your situation. Educate them about what you're going through so they can provide the appropriate support. Sometimes, just having someone listen can significantly affect how you feel. Additionally, community resources like workshops or local non-profit organizations can offer support and information to help you navigate your recovery. These resources often provide access to various activities and events that can enrich your healing process, allowing you to rebuild your social life and regain confidence in your ability to forge healthy relationships.

Incorporating books, online resources, and workshops into your healing process can significantly enhance your understanding and coping strategies. For instance, books written by experts in the field or those who have survived toxic relationships can offer insights and guidance that resonate with your experiences. Online resources, including blogs, podcasts, and forums, provide accessible tools and a platform for connecting with others who share similar experiences. On the other hand, workshops can offer both learning and interactive experiences that help you apply new knowledge in real-world scenarios, facilitating more profound healing and growth.

Monitoring your progress and setbacks is essential for maintaining momentum in your healing journey. Keeping a journal can be particularly useful here, as it allows you to document your feelings, thoughts, and experiences over time. This record helps process emotions and identify patterns and triggers you may need to address further. Recognizing and celebrating small victories is crucial as it reinforces your progress and motivates you to continue. Similarly, understanding and accepting setbacks as part of the healing process can prevent feelings of discouragement and help you maintain a realistic perspective on your recovery.

By engaging with these self-help strategies, you empower yourself to take active steps toward healing. This approach not only aids in recovering from the past but also in building a robust foundation for future relationships. Through self-education, peer support, guided reflection, and leveraging community resources, you equip yourself with the tools necessary to navigate out of the shadows of toxic relationships and into a brighter, healthier future.

7.5 The Role of Spirituality in Healing from Toxicity

In the aftermath of a toxic relationship, seeking solace in spirituality can serve as a profound source of comfort, guidance, and renewal. Engaging in various spiritual beliefs and practices, such as meditation, prayer, and structured rituals, offers inner peace and pathways to healing. These practices aid in managing the emotional distress that follows toxic relationships while fostering a deeper connection with oneself and the universe, thus significantly contributing to the recovery process.

For example, meditation enables the cultivation of a state of calm and centeredness, facilitating the clearing of chaotic thoughts and providing a new perspective on past experiences. It encourages sitting with emotions, even the uncomfortable ones, and observing them without judgment, which can be incredibly liberating after a relationship where emotions are often invalidated. Similarly, regardless of religious affiliations, prayer can provide a sense of being heard and supported by a higher power, offering comfort during moments of despair and loneliness. Rituals, involving acts such as lighting candles or chanting, can mark significant moments in the healing journey, aiding in letting go of bitterness and embracing a new phase of life. These rituals provide a tangible way to enact internal changes and can be compelling.

Incorporating these spiritual practices into daily routines can be easily manageable. It can be as simple as starting the day with a five-minute meditation or prayer, expressing gratitude, or seeking strength for the day ahead. Alternatively, setting aside a specific time each week for a ritual that resonates with one's spiritual beliefs can also be effective. Consistency and intention behind the practice are key, and over time, these moments of spiritual connection can become vital touchstones, significantly enhancing overall well-being and resilience.

The role of spiritual communities in supporting individuals healing from toxic relationships cannot be overstated. Whether based around organized religions, spiritual teachings, or less structured spiritual beliefs, these communities provide a sense of belonging and collective wisdom to draw upon. Engaging with a community that shares one's spiritual values can offer validation and understanding, which are crucial during recovery. Shared experiences within these groups can lead to deep, meaningful connections with others who may provide emotional support and practical advice based on their journeys through healing.

Respecting diverse spiritual perspectives is crucial, as spirituality can play different roles in each person's life and recovery process. Encouraging an open, inclusive environment where various spiritual practices and beliefs are respected can significantly enhance healing, fostering a more profound understanding among individuals. This respect enriches the communal support system and allows a broader range of experiences and insights to be shared and valued.

In essence, spirituality offers a unique and powerful set of tools for those recovering from toxic relationships. Whether through meditation, prayer, rituals, or the supportive networks found in spiritual communities, these practices provide a pathway to healing nurturing both the mind and the soul. By integrating spirituality into daily life and embracing its communal support, individuals equip themselves with the resources to heal deeply and fully, transforming their experience into empowerment and renewal.

7.6 The Impact of Gender Roles on Recovery Dynamics

In the intricate process of recovering from toxic relationships, understanding the influence of gender roles is pivotal. Society often imposes different expectations and stereotypes on different genders, shaping their experiences and responses to toxic relationships. For instance, men are frequently discouraged from expressing vulnerability, which can hinder their ability to seek help or openly discuss their emotional pain. Women, on the other hand, might find themselves facing societal pressures to nurture or 'fix' their partners, potentially trapping them in harmful cycles of codependency and sacrifice. These gender-specific challenges can significantly impact recovery dynamics, making addressing and navigating these barriers effectively essential.

To overcome these gender-specific challenges, it's crucial to foster an environment of empowerment that encourages breaking free from traditional gender roles that may perpetuate toxicity. For men, this means challenging the stigma around expressing vulnerability and seeking emotional support. Creating safe spaces where men can share their experiences without judgment can help dismantle these barriers. Workshops, support groups, and even online forums dedicated to men's mental health can play a significant role in changing these narratives, providing both support and validation that emotional expression is a strength, not a weakness. For women, empowerment involves affirming their right to set boundaries and prioritize their well-being. Educational programs and resources that focus on self-worth and independence can equip women with the tools needed to recognize and exit toxic dynamics without feeling obligated to repair or endure harmful relationships.

Moreover, the influence of rigid gender roles can extend to non-binary and transgender individuals, who may face unique challenges in toxic relationships, including discrimination and a lack of understanding from others about their identity. Support resources that are inclusive and specifically cater to the needs of transgender and non-binary individuals are essential. These resources should not only offer support for issues related to toxic relationships but also provide a supportive community that respects and understands gender diversity. Training for counselors and support staff in gender inclusivity can also enhance the effectiveness of these resources, ensuring that all individuals feel welcomed and supported.

Educating all genders about the characteristics of healthy, respectful relationships is fundamental to preventing future toxic dynamics. This education should start early, ideally incorporated into school curriculums and community programs, emphasizing the importance of mutual respect, consent, and equality in all relationships. Education initiatives should also address how to identify and safely exit toxic relationships, equipping individuals with the knowledge to protect themselves and others. Furthermore, these educational efforts should strive to be inclusive, acknowledging and respecting the diversity of gender identities and experiences, ensuring everyone receives relevant and practical guidance.

Support resources tailored to specific gender-related needs and challenges are crucial in ensuring that individuals receive the appropriate assistance during their recovery. These resources can range from gender-specific support groups to counseling services that specialize in addressing the psychological impacts of gender-related issues in toxic relationships. Additionally, creating resource directories that provide information on gender-sensitive therapists, legal advisors, and community support initiatives can help individuals easily access the help they need. These directories could be made available in community centers, healthcare facilities, and online, ensuring wide accessibility.

Recognizing the profound impact of gender roles in the dynamics of toxic relationships and recovery is not just about providing support —it's about fostering a deeper understanding and challenging the societal norms that contribute to these issues. By empowering individuals to break free from traditional gender roles, providing inclusive and tailored support resources, and educating all genders on healthy relationship dynamics, we pave the way for more equitable and supportive recovery processes. This comprehensive approach not only aids individuals in healing from past toxic relationships but also cultivates a societal framework that promotes healthy, respectful relationships across all genders.

As we wrap up this chapter on the unique challenges and strategies related to gender in recovering from toxic relationships, remember that understanding and addressing these issues is vital for holistic healing and prevention. By acknowledging the complex interplay of gender roles and toxic dynamics, we enable more effective and compassionate recovery processes that honor each individual's experience. This reflection sets the stage for our next chapter, which will explore advanced psychological strategies to further empower you on your path to recovery and renewal.

EIGHT

Empowerment and Future-Proofing Your Love Life

Have you ever paused to reflect on the blueprint of your romantic experiences, noticing a pattern, perhaps a blueprint, that seems to sketch out each relationship you've entered? It's no coincidence that the ghosts of relationships past often whisper into the decisions of the present, shaping how and whom we love. In this chapter, we delve into crafting a personal philosophy for love that resonates deeply with your core values and life experiences, guiding you toward healthier, more fulfilling relationships.

8.1 Building a Personal Philosophy for Healthy Love

Define Personal Love Philosophy

Creating your philosophy of love is akin to drawing your map in the vast landscape of human connection. This philosophy isn't just about who you choose to love but how and why you engage in love the way you do. Begin by asking yourself what "healthy love" means to you. Is it a partnership that champions mutual growth and respect? Is it a bond where communication flows as freely as laughter? Or is it a relationship that offers a sturdy foundation of trust and support? Defining this helps anchor your emotional and relational decisions, steering you clear from the reefs of toxicity that may have trapped you before.

Influence of Past Experiences

Every relationship, with its joys and challenges, deposits layers of learning and unlearning, shaping your emotional and romantic blueprint. Reflect on these past experiences. What patterns emerge? Perhaps you've consistently given more than you've received or walled off emotions to safeguard your heart. Understanding these patterns isn't about fostering regret but about gaining clarity. Each relationship offers fertile ground for lessons, helping you refine your philosophy over time. For instance, an experience of betrayal might heighten the importance of trust in your philosophy, guiding you toward relationships where transparency is valued and exemplified.

Aligning Philosophy with Actions

With a philosophy in hand, the next step is ensuring your romantic choices align with this vision. This alignment is crucial as it turns your philosophy from concept to action, influencing your choice of partners and how you navigate challenges within relationships. For example, if your philosophy prioritizes mutual respect, actively choosing partners who demonstrate respect in all aspects of their lives becomes a non-negotiable. Similarly, if communication is a cornerstone of your philosophy, engaging in practices that enhance openness and understanding, like regular relationship check-ins, becomes essential. This alignment fosters relationship satisfaction and stability and protects against dissonance when actions and ideals do not match.

Revising and Adapting Philosophy

As with all aspects of life, change is constant in personal growth and relationships. Your philosophy of love will need revisiting and refining as you evolve and learn more about yourself and the nature of relationships. This flexibility allows your philosophy to remain relevant and supportive as your life experiences broaden. You may discover a more profound value of independence than you previously appreciated or encounter a facet of compatibility you had underestimated. Allowing your philosophy to evolve this way ensures it continually serves as a reliable compass, guiding your heart through the complexities of love and life.

Interactive Element: Reflective Journaling Prompts

- What three qualities do you see as most essential in a healthy relationship?
- Reflect on a past relationship: what lesson did it teach you about what you truly value in partnerships?
- How have your actions in recent relationships aligned with your philosophy of love? Where have they diverged?
- List three ways to update your love philosophy based on your relationship goals and personal growth.

By actively engaging with these prompts, you deepen your understanding of your romantic needs and desires and equip yourself to make choices that align with your true self. This ongoing process of reflection and adaptation is critical to building and sustaining relationships that survive and thrive, enriching your life with love that is both transformative and true to who you are.

8.2 Techniques for Enhancing Self-Reliance in Emotional Health

In the tapestry of relationships, emotional self-reliance is like the strong, vibrant thread that holds the pattern intact without overshadowing the other colors. Emphasizing the importance of being emotionally self-reliant means recognizing that you enter relationships by choice and not out of a deficit need for completion. This concept doesn't suggest emotional isolation; instead, it proposes a form of emotional maturity where you can fulfill your own emotional needs and not use relationships as crutches. When you are emotionally self-reliant, your relationships are more about sharing your completeness than completing each other. This shift enhances personal satisfaction and stabilizes your relationships, making them less about need and more about mutual growth and happiness.

Developing emotional resilience is fundamental to achieving this state of self-reliance. Techniques such as cognitive reframing are invaluable here. Cognitive reframing involves changing your perspective on a situation to manage your emotional reactions effectively. For instance, instead of viewing a partner's busy schedule as neglect, you can reframe it to appreciate their dedication to their goals, supporting them while valuing your time to pursue personal interests. Stress management is another crucial skill, encompassing a range of practices from structured relaxation techniques like guided imagery or progressive muscle relaxation to simple daily activities like mindful walking or engaging in hobbies that relax and rejuvenate you. Emotional regulation skills are also critical; they help you manage and respond to your emotions in a way consistent with your values and goals. Deep breathing exercises, meditation, and journaling can help maintain emotional equilibrium.

Linking effective self-care practices to enhanced emotional self-reliance involves incorporating activities that boost emotional independence into your routine. Regular physical activity, for instance, not only improves physical health but also enhances mood and emotional well-being, reducing symptoms of depression and anxiety. Engaging in social activities can expand your emotional support network, reducing over-reliance on your partner for social satisfaction. Creative pursuits like painting, writing, or playing music can be particularly therapeutic, allowing for the expression and processing of emotions constructively. These activities encourage a robust sense of self and personal fulfillment, which is essential to emotional self-reliance.

Balancing interdependence and self-reliance in relationships is akin to walking a tightrope where both ends need equal weighting to avoid a fall. It involves understanding that while emotional support from a partner is valuable, relying solely on them for your emotional stability is precarious. Healthy interdependence allows for mutual support without dependency, where both partners benefit from the relationship's emotional resources without feeling depleted. This balance requires open communication about needs and boundaries, regular self-reflection to assess personal emotional health, and a commitment to personal growth. For example, you can actively discuss with your partner how you can support each other's goals while ensuring time for individual pursuits. This kind of dialogue fosters an environment where both partners feel empowered to contribute to the relationship while thriving individually.

Nurturing this delicate balance between self-reliance and interdependence paves the way for relationships that are not just enduring but also enriching. This equilibrium enhances romantic relationships and improves interactions across all areas of life, from friendships to professional connections. Embracing emotional self-reliance does not mean distancing yourself from emotional connections but instead entering them with a sense of wholeness and stability, ready to share your life rather than relying on someone else to complete it.

8.3 The Role of Community and Support Groups in Sustaining Recovery

In the landscape of emotional recovery and personal growth, the role of a supportive community or group cannot be overstated. Imagine these groups as gardens where individuals with unique stories of struggle and recovery come together to share, nurture, and grow. The benefits of such engagement are manifold. Firstly, shared experiences foster a deep sense of understanding and solidarity. Knowing you are not alone in your struggles can be incredibly comforting and can reduce the isolation often felt during recovery. This shared space usually becomes a fertile ground for emotional support, where empathy and encouragement flow freely, helping you to navigate the ups and downs of healing with greater resilience.

Moreover, support groups provide a structure of accountability that can be crucial in maintaining commitment to recovery goals. Members can motivate each other to stay on track, share strategies that have worked for them, and gently remind each other of their progress, even when it feels insubstantial. This accountability is not about imposing strict checks but nurturing a supportive environment where every small step forward is recognized and celebrated. Such groups can significantly amplify your recovery efforts, providing a safety net and a lift toward greater emotional heights.

Finding the right support group or community is pivotal and can influence the trajectory of your recovery journey. Start by identifying what you need most at your current stage of recovery. Are you seeking emotional understanding, practical recovery tips, or a blend of both? Once your needs are precise, explore options in your local community and online. Many organizations offer groups focused on specific recovery themes, such as surviving emotional abuse, navigating life after divorce, or rebuilding self-esteem. Attend a few sessions to see if the group's dynamics and the facilitator's approach resonate with your values and recovery needs. You must feel safe and valued; your contributions should be respected and your boundaries upheld.

The choice between online and in-person support groups can also impact your recovery experience. In-person groups offer a tangible sense of connection, the warmth of physical presence, and non-verbal communication cues, which can be very reassuring. Conversely, online groups provide flexibility and accessibility, which can be a boon if geographical or time constraints are a factor in your life. They also offer anonymity, making sharing sensitive or deeply personal issues easier. However, online interactions sometimes need more depth of connection than face-to-face interactions foster and may pose challenges in building lasting relationships. Consider your lifestyle, personal comfort with digital communication, and the nature of support you are seeking when making this choice.

Active participation in these groups plays a crucial role in maximizing their benefits. While it's perfectly okay to spend initial sessions mostly listening and acclimating, contributing actively can significantly enhance your sense of empowerment and belonging over time. Sharing your experiences and recovery strategies helps others and reinforces your progress and learning. Moreover, articulating your journey can provide new insights into your experiences, deepening your understanding and appreciation of how far you've come. Support groups thrive on reciprocity; the more you put in, the more you and your peers benefit.

Engaging with a community or support group during recovery is not just about receiving support—it's about building a network of relationships that can transform your healing process. These groups offer a space to learn, share, and connect, turning the often lonely road to recovery into a path of shared journeys and mutual growth. Whether online or in person, the right group can provide a powerful catalyst for healing, offering you tools, empathy, and the encouragement needed to move towards a healthier, more fulfilled self.

8.4 Using Personal Stories of Recovery to Inspire Others

The tapestry of our lives is woven with stories, each thread colored with our experiences and emotions. In the context of recovery, these personal narratives are not just reflections of our past; they are beacons that can light the way for others navigating similar dark waters. The power of personal storytelling lies in its ability to connect, resonate, and inspire. When you share your journey of overcoming the challenges of a toxic relationship, it does more than recount your struggles and triumphs; it offers hope and possible solutions to those who hear it.

However, sharing personal stories, especially those involving emotional vulnerability, requires careful consideration to ensure you are not compromising your privacy and emotional well-being. It is crucial to set boundaries around what you are comfortable disclosing. Decide which parts of your story are public and reserved for more private settings. Rehearse your story alone or with a trusted friend to identify areas that feel too raw or personal to share openly. This exercise can also help you refine the message you want to convey, focusing on the insights and growth you experienced rather than only the painful aspects.

Choosing the right platform for sharing your story is equally important. Each platform offers different interactions and reaches diverse audiences. Blogs and personal websites provide a space to elaborate on your story in detail, accompanied by reflections and learnings. This format also allows readers to engage with your story at their own pace, which can be particularly beneficial for those reflecting on their experiences. Social media platforms, while more public, can amplify your narrative's reach, connecting you with a global audience quickly. These platforms are ideal for sharing shorter, more impactful elements of your story, possibly through posts or videos highlighting critical moments of your recovery journey.

Speaking engagements and podcasts offer more intimate settings where the nuances of your voice and emotion can deeply engage the audience. These platforms are particularly effective for connecting on a human level, as they allow for real-time interaction and enable you to respond to questions, providing further insights based on your audience's needs. When choosing a platform, consider your comfort level with public speaking, your desired reach, and the level of personal interaction you are ready to handle.

The impact of sharing your recovery story extends beyond inspiring others; it also significantly reinforces your journey of healing and self-understanding. Articulating your experiences helps you to process emotions and events that might have been too complex or painful to address internally. It also offers you a new perspective on your growth, highlighting strengths and resilience you may have yet to acknowledge fully. Furthermore, sharing your story publicly can transform your recovery into a mission, providing a sense of purpose and achievement. This transformation solidifies your progress and empowers you to continue moving forward, driven by the knowledge that your experiences are helping others to heal and grow.

In sharing your story, you weave your thread into the larger human tapestry, turning your personal experiences into universal lessons of resilience and hope. This act of sharing not only enriches the lives of others but also deepens your understanding and appreciation of your journey. It is a powerful testament to the strength of the human spirit and the profound connection we share through our stories. As you consider opening up about your path to recovery, remember that your voice can uplift, educate, and inspire, turning even the most painful experiences into beacons of hope for others.

8.5 Innovations in Therapy and Personal Development for Relationship Health

As we navigate the evolving landscape of personal development and therapy, exploring how cutting-edge innovations can transform how we approach relationship health is thrilling. Imagine entering a virtual reality scenario where you can practice difficult conversations with a digital version of your partner, honed by artificial intelligence, to respond like they would in real life. This is just one example of how technology like virtual reality therapy and AI-powered mental health tools revolutionize our approach to developing healthier relationships. These technologies offer immersive experiences and data-driven insights that were unimaginable a decade ago, providing new pathways to understand and improve our interactions with others.

Integrating these advanced technologies into your personal development plan can seem daunting, but it's about tailoring these tools to serve your unique needs and relationship goals. For instance, virtual reality therapy can be an excellent tool for those who struggle with conflict resolution, offering a safe space to navigate and practice complex interpersonal dynamics without real-world repercussions. AI-powered apps can help track mood and emotional health, providing personalized insights and prompts to help you manage stress and anxiety about your relationship dynamics. The key is to start small—incorporate one technological tool that addresses your most pressing relationship challenge and gradually expand as you become more comfortable and notice improvements.

Evaluating the effectiveness of these new therapies and technologies is crucial to ensure they genuinely contribute to your growth. Start by setting clear, measurable goals for what you hope to achieve through their use, such as improved communication, reduced conflict, or better emotional regulation. Use these objectives as a baseline to assess progress over time. Additionally, consider maintaining a journal where you can note any changes in your relationship dynamics or personal well-being that may correlate with using these technologies. Feedback from your partner can also provide invaluable insights into how these innovations impact your relationship from both sides. If the technology offers analytics or reporting features, use these tools to track trends and patterns that can inform further adjustments to your approach.

Addressing ethical considerations is also essential when incorporating advanced technologies into therapy and personal development. Informed consent is a cornerstone of ethical practice, ensuring you fully understand how these technologies work, what data they collect, and how that information is used. Privacy is another critical consideration, especially with tools that collect and analyze personal data. Verify that any technology you use complies with relevant privacy laws and standards and that there is transparency about data usage. Furthermore, the implications of dependency on technology for emotional management and relationship health should be considered. Using these tools to enhance your skills and insights is essential, not replace the fundamental human elements of empathy, connection, and emotional intimacy.

As you explore these innovative technologies, remember they are tools designed to enhance your journey toward healthier relationships. They offer exciting possibilities to deepen your understanding of yourself and your partner, providing tailored approaches that can adjust to your evolving needs. Whether through virtual scenarios, AI-driven insights, or other emerging technologies, the landscape of therapy and personal development is expanding rapidly, offering new avenues to enhance how we connect and thrive in relationships.

8.6 Future Trends in Dating and Relationships: Staying Ahead

As we gaze toward the horizon of dating and relationships, it's evident that the landscape is transforming rapidly, influenced heavily by technological advancements and shifting societal norms. Digital platforms have revolutionized how we connect, bringing a new era where finding a date is as simple as swiping a screen. However, this ease of connection brings complexities, as the digital realm often blurs the lines between genuine intimacy and superficial interaction. Moreover, societal shifts towards more fluid definitions of relationships challenge traditional models, urging us to reconsider what commitment and love look like in the modern age.

Navigating these changes effectively requires not just awareness but a strategic approach. As digital interactions become the norm, it's crucial to maintain a critical eye, distinguishing meaningful connections from transient digital interactions. Prioritize depth and quality in your communications, seeking to establish connections that transcend the superficial layers often promoted by online platforms. For instance, instead of cycling through quick chat exchanges, propose video calls or meet-ups that foster a more genuine connection. Additionally, as societal norms evolve, keeping an open mind and continuously educating yourself about diverse relationship models can enhance your understanding and acceptance, allowing you to engage more profoundly with potential partners who might view or experience love differently than you do.

Predicting the future of dating and relationships involves acknowledging the growing role of technology not just as a medium of connection and a tool for enhancing relationship quality. We might see increased use of algorithms to predict compatibility more accurately, virtual reality setups that allow people to share experiences in real-time despite physical distances, or AI-driven counseling services that provide relationship advice tailored to individual needs. Preparing for these changes means staying informed about technological advancements and critically assessing how they can enhance or hinder your relationship goals. Embrace technology that fosters genuine connection and growth in your relationships while being wary of tools that may lead to increased isolation or superficial interactions.

The importance of continuous learning and adaptation in personal and romantic life cannot be overstated. As a relationships' dynamics evolve, so must our approaches to managing and nurturing them. Commit to lifelong learning about relationship skills, emotional intelligence, and technological trends impacting social interactions. This continuous education will not only help you adapt to changes but also enable you to thrive in a dating world that is perpetually evolving. Engage with resources that challenge your understanding and expand your perspectives on relationships. Workshops, books, and podcasts on modern relationships and technology's role within them can provide valuable insights and strategies for adapting to the changing landscape.

In conclusion, as we wrap up this exploration into the future trends of dating and relationships, it's clear that staying ahead requires a blend of openness, critical engagement, and proactive adaptation. By understanding and integrating these emerging trends, you equip yourself to navigate the evolving landscape of love and connection with confidence and insight. As we move forward, remember that the core of healthy relationships—respect, communication, and genuine connection—remains unchanged, even as the platforms and norms around them evolve. Let's carry these values with us as we step into the dynamic future of dating and relationships, ready to embrace the challenges and opportunities.

Conclusion

As we draw this transformative journey to a close, I want to reflect on the significant strides we've made together through the pages of this book. We embarked on a profound exploration of healing from toxic relationships. Remember the following text:

This journey has been about understanding the complex nature of our interactions, breaking free, and fostering a future filled with healthy, respectful, and loving relationships. It's been about rediscovering oneself, reclaiming self-love, and respecting the boundaries that safeguard our well-being.

Self-love and self-respect are the keys to recovery and future happiness in relationships. These are not just buzzwords but the foundation of your liberation from toxic cycles. By embracing these principles, you will have the strength to break free from damaging patterns and attract relationships that honor and enrich you.

Throughout this book, we've unpacked key strategies that pave the way for healing and empowerment. Setting clear boundaries, engaging in consistent self-care, boosting your emotional intelligence, and leaning into supporting a compassionate community are steps and leaps toward a brighter, healthier relational future. We discussed the transformative power of developing a personal philosophy for love and the critical role of emotional self-reliance. These essential tools empower you to maintain the course in the face of future challenges.

The shared personal stories and the community's collective wisdom underscore the healing power of solidarity and shared experiences. Please seek out and contribute to these supportive networks. Your journey and your voice have the power to light the way for others navigating similar paths.

I urge you to take that courageous first step toward your recovery and empowerment. Apply the strategies we've explored, seek professional guidance, and immerse yourself in communities that uplift your spirit. Remember, a thousand-mile journey begins with a single step, and today marks a pivotal starting point.

As we look ahead, let's hold on to hope and optimism. Recovery from toxic relationships is not just a possibility—it's a reality for many, and it can be your reality, too. A future filled with healthy, fulfilling relationships is not just a dream; it's within your reach, waiting for you to grasp it with both hands.

The path of personal growth and learning is never-ending. I encourage you to remain committed to your self-evolution, stay abreast of the latest dating and relationship trends, and continue to adapt and grow. Life is a continuous learning journey, and each step forward enriches your experience and broadens your horizons.

Share your journey, your successes, and your lessons. Whether through social media, writing, or speaking engagements, your story can inspire and support others seeking light amid darkness. Let your journey be a beacon for others, just as the stories shared in this book have illuminated your path.

Thank you for trusting me to guide you through this transformative process. Your determination to seek a better, healthier life is inspiring. It has been a privilege to walk alongside you in this journey of healing and rediscovery. Now let's move forward with courage, hope, and an unyielding belief in our capacity to love and be loved in the healthiest ways possible.

Let's continue to grow, learn, and thrive in our relationships and life. Thank you for sharing this journey with me.

Bonus Worksheet

Objective: This worksheet aims to help you break free from a toxic relationship cycle, live authentically, love fully, and rediscover yourself.

Section 1: Recognizing the Toxic Patterns

Identify Toxic Behaviors: List specific behaviors or patterns in your relationship that feel toxic or harmful.

_____

_____

_____

_____

_____

_____

Example: Gaslighting, manipulation, constant criticism.

Impact Assessment: How did these toxic behaviors affect you emotionally, mentally, and physically?

_____

_____

_____

_____

_____

_____

_____

Example: Increased anxiety, self-doubt, loss of self-esteem.

Personal Accountability:

Reflect on any behaviors or patterns you might have contributed to
or accepted.

_____

_____

_____

_____

_____

_____

_____

Example: Tolerating disrespect, neglecting your own needs.

Section 2: Breaking the Cycle

Set Boundaries: Identify at least three boundaries you need to set to protect yourself.

_____

_____

_____

_____

_____

_____

Example: Limit or cease contact, avoid engaging in arguments.

Develop a Plan: Create a step-by-step plan for how to distance yourself from the toxic relationship.

_____

_____

_____

_____

_____

_____

Example: Plan a safe exit strategy, seek support from friends or professionals.

Self-Care Practices: List five self-care activities that help you feel grounded and centered.

_____

_____

_____

_____

_____

_____

Example: Journaling, exercise, meditation.

Section 3: Living Authentically

Self-Discovery: Write down your core values and beliefs that define who you are.

_____

_____

_____

_____

_____

_____

Example: Honesty, creativity, compassion.

Passion and Interests: List activities or hobbies that bring you joy and fulfillment.

_____

_____

_____

_____

_____

_____

_____

Example: Painting, hiking, reading.

Authentic Goals: Set three personal goals that align with your true self and aspirations.

_____

_____

_____

_____

_____

_____

_____

_____

_____

Example: Pursue a new career, develop a healthy routine, build meaningful relationships. Be specific.

Section 4: Loving Fully

Section 5: Rediscovering Yourself

Make sure to scan this QR Code
to get the rest of this Work Sheet and
Free Workbook

Free Workbook +

References

1. Bretherton, I. (1992). The origins of attachment theory: John Bowlby and Mary Ainsworth. *Developmental Psychology, 28*(5), 759-775. Retrieved from https://psycnet.apa.org/record/1993-01038-001
2. Luo, Y., & Gao, Y. (2023). The relationship between childhood emotional neglect and adult depression: The mediating role of self-esteem and emotional regulation. *Frontiers in Psychology, 14*. Retrieved from https://www.ncbi.nlm.nih.gov/pmc/articles/PMC10037214/
3. Groh, A. M., Fearon, R. P., Bakermans-Kranenburg, M. J., van IJzendoorn, M. H., Steele, R. D., & Roisman, G. I. (2017). Caregiver sensitivity and consistency and children's prior attachment: A meta-analysis using individual participant data. *Attachment & Human Development, 20*(6), 558-581. Retrieved from https://www.ncbi.nlm.nih.gov/pmc/articles/PMC6092938/
4. Alberts, N. M., Hadjistavropoulos, H. D., & Dear, B. F. (2021). Anxious attachment improves and is predicted by anxiety sensitivity in internet-based, guided self-help cognitive behavioral treatment for panic disorder. *Journal of Anxiety Disorders, 79*. Retrieved from https://pubmed.ncbi.nlm.nih.gov/34410764/
5. American Psychological Association. (n.d.). What is cognitive behavioral therapy? Retrieved from https://www.apa.org/ptsd-guideline/patients-and-families/cognitive-behavioral
6. Verywell Mind. (2022). Self-soothing techniques for anxiety. Retrieved from https://www.verywellmind.com/how-to-self-soothe-when-coping-with-anxiety-5199606
7. Mindspo. (2023, July 6). How we healed an anxious attachment style and created a secure relationship. Retrieved from https://mindspo.com/2023/07/06/how-we-healed-an-anxious-attachment-style/
8. Tsumura, T., Matsunaga, M., & Sakurai, S. (2019). Brief mindfulness meditation improves emotion processing: An ERP study. *Frontiers in Human Neuroscience, 13*. Retrieved from https://www.ncbi.nlm.nih.gov/pmc/articles/PMC6795685/
9. Riley, C. (2015). Childhood trauma and adult interpersonal relationship problems: The role of attachment and emotion regulation. *Journal of Traumatic Stress, 28*(1), 41-51. Retrieved from https://www.ncbi.nlm.nih.gov/pmc/articles/PMC4304140/

10. Psych Central. (n.d.). The 3 basic principles of cognitive behavioral therapy. Retrieved from https://psychcentral.com/pro/the-basic-principles-of-cognitive-behavior-therapy

11. Positive Psychology. (n.d.). Inner child healing: 35 practical tools for growing beyond trauma. Retrieved from https://positivepsychology.com/inner-child-healing/

12. Goldin, P. R., & Gross, J. J. (2014). Mindfulness and emotion regulation: Insights from neuroimaging. *Psychiatric Clinics of North America, 37*(1), 3-11. Retrieved from https://www.ncbi.nlm.nih.gov/pmc/articles/PMC5337506/

13. StatPearls. (2022). Therapeutic communication. Retrieved from https://www.ncbi.nlm.nih.gov/books/NBK567775/

14. American Psychological Association. (n.d.). What is cognitive behavioral therapy? Retrieved from https://www.apa.org/ptsd-guideline/patients-and-families/cognitive-behavioral

15. PsychAlive. (2021). Why is honesty so important in a relationship? Retrieved from https://www.psychalive.org/why-is-honesty-so-important-in-a-relationship/

16. Positive Psychology. (n.d.). Conflict resolution in relationships & couples: 5 strategies. Retrieved from https://positivepsychology.com/conflict-resolution-relationships/

17. Hofmann, S. G., Asnaani, A., Vonk, I. J., Sawyer, A. T., & Fang, A. (2012). The efficacy of cognitive behavioral therapy: A review of meta-analyses. *Cognitive Therapy and Research, 36*(5), 427-440. Retrieved from https://www.ncbi.nlm.nih.gov/pmc/articles/PMC3584580/

18. Choosing Therapy. (2022). Fear of abandonment: Why it happens & how to overcome it. Retrieved from https://www.choosingtherapy.com/fear-of-abandonment/

19. Surf Office. (2022). 30 trust-building exercises and activities for teams. Retrieved from https://www.surfoffice.com/blog/trust-building-exercises

20. Arnett, J. J. (2000). Relationship influences on exploration in adulthood: Evidence from a national study of American adults. *Journal of Social and Personal Relationships, 17*(5), 667-683. Retrieved from https://www.ncbi.nlm.nih.gov/pmc/articles/PMC2805473/

21. Medical News Today. (2021). How to fix an anxious attachment style. Retrieved from https://www.medicalnewstoday.com/articles/how-to-fix-anxious-attachment-style

22. Andrews, G., Cuijpers, P., Craske, M. G., McEvoy, P., & Titov, N. (2010). Cognitive-behavioral therapy for anxiety disorders: A meta-analysis of randomized placebo-controlled trials. *World Psychiatry, 9*(4), 197-210. Retrieved from https://www.ncbi.nlm.nih.gov/pmc/articles/PMC4610618/

23. Verywell Mind. (2022). Secure attachment: Signs, benefits, and how to cultivate it. Retrieved from https://www.verywellmind.com/secure-attachment-signs-benefits-and-how-to-cultivate-it-8628802

24. Greater Good Science Center. (2021). Five science-backed strategies to build resilience. Retrieved from https://greatergood.berkeley.edu/article/item/five_science_backed_strategies_to_build_resilience

25. American Psychological Association. (n.d.). What is cognitive behavioral therapy? Retrieved from https://www.apa.org/ptsd-guideline/patients-and-families/cognitive-behavioral

26. Hofmann, S. G., & Gómez, A. F. (2017). Mindfulness-based interventions for anxiety and depression. *Psychiatric Clinics of North America, 40*(4), 739-749. Retrieved from https://www.ncbi.nlm.nih.gov/pmc/articles/PMC5679245/

27. Marriage.com. (2022). 6 ways on how to build trust in long-distance relationships. Retrieved from https://www.marriage.com/advice/relationship/ways-on-how-to-build-trust-in-long-distance-relationships/

28. Norton Healthcare. (2021). Art therapy patient shares stories of hope and healing. Retrieved from https://nortonhealthcare.com/news/art-therapy-patient-shares-stories-of-hope-and-healing/

29. Greater Good Science Center. (2015). How gratitude changes you and your brain. Retrieved from https://greatergood.berkeley.edu/article/item/how_gratitude_changes_you_and_your_brain

30. Andrews, G., Cuijpers, P., Craske, M. G., McEvoy, P., & Titov, N. (2010). Cognitive-behavioral therapy for anxiety disorders: A meta-analysis of randomized placebo-controlled trials. *World Psychiatry, 9*(4), 197-210. Retrieved from https://www.ncbi.nlm.nih.gov/pmc/articles/PMC4610618/

31. Psychology Today. (2021). The power of rituals. Retrieved from https://www.psychologytoday.com/us/blog/dont-forget-the-basil/202104/the-power-of-rituals

32. JSTOR. (2007). Impacts of lifelong learning upon emotional resilience and psychological well-being. *International Journal of Lifelong Education, 26*(3), 339-354. Retrieved from https://www.jstor.org/stable/4127165

Made in the USA
Las Vegas, NV
29 December 2024

15566788R00085